NOLS
Wilderness Ethics

NOLS
Wilderness Ethics

Valuing and Managing Wild Places

revisions and new text by

Jennifer Lamb and Glenn Goodrich

original text by

Susan Chadwick Brame and Chad Henderson

STACKPOLE
BOOKS

Published by
STACKPOLE BOOKS
5067 Ritter Road
Mechanicsburg, PA 17055
www.stackpolebooks.com

Printed in the United States of America

This is a revised and updated edition of *An Introduction to Wildland Ethics and Management* by Susan Chadwick Brame and Chad Henderson, originally published by the National Outdoor Leadership School in 1992.

Cover design by Caroline Stover
Cover photograph by John McConnell

Library of Congress Cataloguing-in-Publication Data

Lamb, Jennifer.
   NOLS wilderness ethics and management : valuing and managing wild places / revisions and new text by Jennifer Lamb and Glenn Goodrich ; original text by Susan Chadwick Brame and Chad Henderson.
      p. cm.
   Rev. ed. of: Introduction to wildland ethics & management / Susan Chadwick Brame and Chad Henderson. c1992.
   Includes bibliographical references.
   ISBN-13: 978-0-8117-3254-3
   ISBN-10: 0-8117-3254-1
   1. Wilderness areas—Management. 2. Wilderness areas—United States —Management. 3. Wilderness areas—Moral and ethical aspects. I. Goodrich, Glenn. II. Brame, Susan Chadwick. Introduction to wildland ethics & management. III. National Outdoor Leadership School (U.S.) IV. Title.
   QH75.B69 2006
   333.78'2—dc22

                                                                    2005030392

Contents

Acknowledgments

We are extraordinarily grateful for the time, energy, and thoughtful perspectives of the many individuals who contributed to this book.

Susan Chadwick Brame and Chad Henderson poured an immense amount of time, research, knowledge, and creativity into writing and publishing the first version of the book, the core of which remains in this updated edition. We thank them for producing such a terrific resource and for making the job of revising it so easy.

Our review committee provided critical input: Dick Paterson, USDA Forest Service, Director, Grey Towers National Historic Site; Darryl Knuffke, The Wilderness Society; Rick Potts, National Park Service National Wilderness Program Manager; Paul Sneed, Prescott College, Environmental Studies Core Faculty and Ph.D. coordinator; John Cederquist, University of Utah, Department of Parks, Recreation and Leisure; Kerry Brophy, NOLS Publications Manager; John Gookin, NOLS Curriculum Manager; and Molly Hampton, NOLS Administration and Partnerships Director.

We also appreciate the ideas and editorial input provided by Rich Brame, Andy Blair, Brad Christensen, Willy Cunningham, John Gans, Roger Kaye, Bridget Lyons, Karen Paisley, Bruce Palmer, Shannon Rochelle, and Rudy Schuster.

Lastly, we thank our families, friends, and the thousands of NOLS students and co-workers with whom we've had the good fortune to travel, teach, and learn in wilderness. Their contributions were ever-present during the development of this book.

Foreword

by Paul G. Sneed

I was fortunate enough to be born and raised in the American West, surrounded by what seemed an abundance of wilderness and wildlife. Like Aldo Leopold, I was glad to never have been "young without wild country to be young in." However, beyond my own immediate enjoyment of the wildlands, I have come to understand the profound societal value of wildness. I now believe that human survival depends on us learning to live sustainably on Earth and that in order to do this we need, in the words of Thomas Berry, "to appreciate the spontaneities found in every form of existence in the natural world, spontaneities that we associate with the wild—that which is uncontrolled by human dominance." Moreover, we need all the help we can get with educating our fellow humans about the centrality and sacredness of the wild.

These days, as I gaze south from my home in central Montana toward the magnificent mountain ranges of the Absaroka-Beartooth Wilderness, I give thanks for dedicated conservation advocates like Bob Marshall and Howard Zahniser, who worked tirelessly for years to ensure the final passage of the Wilderness Act in 1964. Nevertheless, forty years later the future of wildness in America still seems uncertain. For example, here in Montana, we have not seen any additional areas designated under the Wilderness Act since 1983. Even more discouraging are the hundreds of anti-environmental actions taken in the last few years by federal politicians and government agencies, such as the recent decision to rescind the "Roadless Rule," which prohibited new roads and industrial development on 58.5 million acres of Forest Service lands. Despite these assaults on our wilderness heritage, I am a perennial optimist who believes, as the polls always show, that the majority of Americans value our public wildlands and want them protected for future generations.

It is this hope for the future, along with my belief in the power of grassroots political action, that leads me to welcome the revision and commercial publication of this concise and user-friendly book on wildland management and ethics. The authors of this second edition, Glenn Goodrich and Jennifer Lamb, have provided an extremely thorough overview that will help the reader navigate the complex maze of laws, policies, and agency structures governing public wildlands management. Equally helpful and useful is their well-balanced discussion of the historical development of and current perspectives on wildland ethics and how they define our relationship with the land. Taken together, the two main themes in this book will be very worthwhile for consideration by anyone desiring to educate people about the value of wildness.

Perhaps more important, this book will be very beneficial to conservationists interested in organizing our citizens to shape policy that will protect our wildland legacy for future generations. I think it is accurate to say that the main mission of Paul Petzoldt, the founder of the National Outdoor Leadership School, was to train competent, compassionate, and courageous leaders, who would cherish and protect our American wilderness. This book makes a valuable contribution to that cause.

Paul G. Sneed is Core Faculty for the Master of Arts Environmental Studies Program and the Program Director of the Ph.D. Program in Sustainability Education at Prescott College in Prescott, Arizona. He also serves on the Board of Directors of six conservation organizations in Arizona and Montana.

Introduction

The idea for this book was born in the spring of 1990, when the Bureau of Land Management asked NOLS to teach a seminar that spurred the development of new curriculum materials. As part of this project, NOLS created a handbook that contained readings on wilderness ethics and management, along with information on expedition planning, first aid, and minimum-impact wilderness skills. While NOLS had published many in-depth resources on most of these topics, we lacked guidance for instructors preparing classes and leading discussions on public lands issues. The first edition of *An Introduction to Wildland Ethics and Management*, an offshoot of the BLM/NOLS handbook, became a popular tool for NOLS staff and students. The new edition of the book updates this valuable resource and makes it available to a growing and dedicated audience of educators, outdoor program managers, recreationists, and all others who share a common interest in our wilderness and public lands.

We believe that every activity on public land should be consciously governed by a thoughtful ethic, and that ethical discourse and management decisions are fundamentally inseparable. A passionate and principled commitment to the wilderness is the foundation of effective, rational participation in public decision-making. Thus, we present wildland ethics and management in the same publication.

The roots of wildland ethics are embedded in the history and culture of our country. From the pioneers who fought unabashedly to show our growing nation the value and necessity of wild places to those who now carry the torch, we have become a land with a proud legacy of wilderness. So too are our wildland management strategies part of our heritage. The founding mission of each federal agency can be traced to individuals who boldly established a vision and purpose for public land. Subsequent changes in social values, economic objectives, attitudes toward wilderness, politics, legislative mandates, and lifestyles have caused the agencies to shift their guiding principles and policies, mirroring the country's priorities.

The purpose of this book is to provide an introduction to some of the concepts related to a wildland ethic and to the decision-making structures that affect public land management. It is not intended to be a comprehensive survey of ethics and land management, nor does it present an official NOLS position on either of these subjects. Ethics are necessarily personal. We hope, however, that this book raises questions, sparks interest and debate, and provides background and knowledge for fostering a relationship with the land and participating in the processes that govern it. Wildlands provide NOLS with spectacular outdoor classrooms. So long as we have the privilege to use these classrooms, we will be actively involved in promoting their thoughtful stewardship.

Susan Chadwick Brame and Chad Henderson
Lander, Wyoming
May 1992

Jennifer Lamb and Glenn Goodrich
Lander, Wyoming
July 2005

A NOTE ON TERMINOLOGY

A variety of terms are used to identify wild places. In this book we use the terms *wildland* and *wilderness* interchangeably and intend them to mean places largely without significant human influence. We substitute a capital "W" in the term *Wilderness* to refer to lands specifically and legally designated by the U.S. Congress for management under the Wilderness Act. These lands often have characteristics similar to undesignated wildlands but serve a unique purpose as defined by the Act.

PART ONE

Wilderness Ethics

There is something magnetic about the attraction of wild places. We feel it while sitting by a quiet stream or on a grand perch at a mountain's summit; every time we hear the bugle of an elk during the fall rut or the raucous cries of a Clark's nutcracker; in the warmth of a campfire and the last glows of a desert sunset. A connection is made with something deep within us, undeniable and ever present. We need wild places and things to refresh this connection, lest it become a dormant remnant of our bond with the earth. And wherever we find wildness, we become, once again, recipients of its tonic—clarity, solace, refreshment, honest toils but unmatched rewards.

What debt do we owe for these gifts? The answer is simple: appreciation. We must gain knowledge of the lands around us, be humble visitors, act with foresight and good intent, use judgment, never take these places for granted, remain compassionate, and care. This is what an ethic is all about. As passengers on this earth, we need to care about it. It's not a difficult thing to do, and the rewards . . . well, the track of a grizzly and the grace of a mountain columbine need no explanation.

1

Defining a Wilderness Ethic

Ethics is a simple word for an intricate moral code—a complex synthesis of human history. Fundamentally, ethics comprise the convergence of choice, judgment, and values. Perhaps therein lies the difficulty. By definition, these three meet within a very subjective realm. Values shape the choices we make when we exercise our judgment, and each individual carries a unique set of values.

In addition to mastering conventional wilderness skills, the ethically minded outdoor traveler must consider his or her relationship with the land.

Devotees of wildlands are a diverse lot with greatly varied motivations—climbing an alluring peak, floating a remote river, fishing an alpine lake, or decompressing from the burdens of a busy world. Whatever the case, wilderness is a domain that requires planning and preparation. Experienced travelers take with them skills needed to be safe and competent, gear to be secure and comfortable, and eagerness that ensures a rewarding trip. But another essential element, affecting the outcome of every venture, is the matter of one's relationship with the land.

Each of us gains a litany of lessons throughout our lifetime, and the camping, climbing, river, and hiking trips one has experienced shape one's ties and interactions with wildlands. How one chooses a campsite or builds a campfire are skills likely learned from a parent or friend. An understanding of ecology comes from a favorite teacher. A reverence for nature blossoms from long walks in serene woods or vibrant nights beneath a blanket of summer stars. Family, environment, education, society, history, religion, and culture all contribute to form the foundation for one's ethic, the guide for one's actions. It is this personal ethic as related to wildlands—one's *wildland ethic*—that defines one's relationship with these lands.

In one application, a wildland ethic lessens the measure of *trace*, the physical impact left on a campsite. In another, the ethic defines how individuals, societies, or governments address issues concerning the management of wildlands. A well-founded ethic also strengthens one's connection to wildlands, enabling the celebration of joy, personal fulfillment, and spiritual contentment commonly found in the wilderness experience.

A personal wildland ethic should represent an arrival at a complex but well-founded set of ideals and behaviors associated with wild places. Pondering the *why* of your behaviors and thoughts is a wonderful exercise in honesty. It is instrumental in living out your responsibility to be a good steward of the places you love. Forming an ethic is a process that is dynamic, thrives on education and experience, and straightforwardly accepts changes in your attitudes and outlooks as you grow throughout your life. Ultimately, wildland ethics are something you become quite comfortable with. In essence, you carry them in your hip pocket and apply them as naturally as tying your boots for the day's journey.

Examining ethics *can* be a complex undertaking—heavy with philosophy and contemplated from every angle imaginable. It's important to keep a focus on why we're concerned with them and why they draw so much discussion. Part 1 of this book considers some of the underpinnings, foundational thought, and contemporary approaches to wildland ethics, and how these affect our interactions with the land. It's not necessary to draw on Aldo Leopold every time you light a campfire or Thoreau each time you enjoy a beautiful sunset. But be assured that their influences are there, perfect contributions to each of our experiences.

In the eighteenth century, German philosopher Immanuel Kant asserted that an individual's moral or ethical conduct is expressed by behaving "in such a way that he can also will that his maxim should become a universal law."[1] Morals beget ethics, which in turn evolve into norms, which are the underpinnings of laws. Aldo Leopold writes that ethics are "social approbation for right actions, social disapproval for wrong actions."[2] But what is right? For wildlands, there has been a great deal of support for letting the land itself determine this and guide us in the "rightness" of our actions. Leopold, in *A Sand County Almanac,* urges us to consider that "a thing is right when it tends to preserve the integrity, stability and beauty of the biotic community. It is wrong when it tends otherwise."[3]

Once a "right" is identified, it follows that there must be a "wrong" and contrasting set of behaviors. In academic circles of wildland or, more broadly, environmental ethics, the boundary between right and wrong is *the* focus of discussion, with debates over intrinsic worth, anthropocentric (human centered) versus biocentric (centered on nonhuman living organisms) values, the rights of biotic (natural, living) beings or communities, sentience (consciousness and awareness), ethnocentrism (a belief in the superiority of certain cultures' practices over those of others), and many other concepts. We are constantly engaged in an effort to correctly identify criteria that help us define whether our actions are the correct ones. Despite ongoing discussion as to what properly defines the ultimate "rightness" of an action, many of us collectively agree that wildlands need our help and attention. In many areas, the amount of visitation to wildlands is increasing, as are ecological and esthetic impacts on this resource. We can see, feel, and measure the scope of damage resulting from loving places to death, underscoring the importance of finding the right ways to interact with these lands.

It is important to view ethics as a whole in the context of today's world. Humans are inextricably connected with the lands of this earth. The reality of human conditions in many societies and cultures may not allow lands to be kept wild, separate from the presence and use of people. The best use of the land often cannot deny providing the resources and refuge that humans need. In such cases, human values identify the right ethical path. Yet in other places the best use is to leave lands without human influence, deeming them wilderness or wild. It is on these lands that the discussion of wildland ethics focuses.

In a congressionally legislated Wilderness Area, our right actions are legally defined by the dictates of the Wilderness Act, where Wilderness is "recognized as an area where the earth and community of life are untrammeled by man, where man himself is a visitor who does not remain."[4] Yet for all wildlands, even outside bounded tracts of Wilderness, a strengthening ecological imperative identifies right and wrong along the course of Leopold's and similar teachings. The advancing science of ecology helps significantly close the gap between guessing which actions are detrimental to the biotic community and knowing via research how to modify human behaviors. Being an active observer of the biotic community aids in developing an ethic that results in making educated choices. As a result, ethics relative to wildlands are becoming more effectively interpreted.

2

Wildlands and People

Man always kills the thing he loves, and so we the pioneers have killed our wilderness. Some say we had to. Be that as it may, I am glad I shall never be young without wild country to be young in. Of what avail are forty freedoms without a blank spot on the map?

—Aldo Leopold

Wilderness is difficult to define satisfactorily because of its historically ephemeral symbolism. Gary Snyder compares the word *wild* to "a gray fox trotting off through the forest, ducking behind bushes, going in and out of sight." He also notes that *wilderness* is commonly defined strictly in negative terms, which tell us what it is *not*. The Random House definition, "a wild and uncultivated region . . . uninhabited or inhabited only by wild animals; a tract of wasteland," is a good example. In contrast, Snyder offers a definition of what wildlands *are:* "a place where the original and potential vegetation and fauna are intact and in full interaction, and the landforms are entirely the result of nonhuman forces."[5] Sociologist Bill Devall and philosopher George Sessions suggest that wilderness might be

TOM BOL

In an era in which all wilderness areas are potentially subject to human contact, wilderness ethics become even more important.

defined as "a landscape or ecosystem that has been minimally disrupted by the intervention of humans, especially the destructive technology of modern societies."[6]

A wildland ethic seeks to define human interactions with lands where nature operates freely, where its needs and seasons are played out on its own terms. But why do we seek out these places? What's the connection? Is there an innate element of being human that urges us to maintain and renew our bond with the natural world?

The fact that wildlands have been an element of human cultures throughout history—sought out or shunned, feared or revered—suggests that there is a con-

FREDRIK NORRSELL

The revegetation that follows a forest fire is one example of an ecological process taking place outside of human influence.

nection. We have an inherent need to explore and understand the world around us. We seek to comprehend where we really do fit in on this earth, and what our connection is with nature's workings. In essence, we want to fully discover and understand our niche.

ECOLOGY: KNOWLEDGE AND FORESIGHT

Though it seems well fixed in our array of sciences, ecology is, in reality, a newcomer on the scene. It is a rich confluence of scientific disciplines that examine ecosystems by studying the myriad interrelationships between organisms and their environment. In application, ecology has only begun to show the importance of the parts to the whole: the role fire plays, the effects of acid rain or nonnative species. The interconnectedness of natural systems has shown that pushing in one place elicits a response in another. Not surprisingly, the more we examine things, the more complex they appear and the more incomplete our knowledge seems.

Wilderness lands are often associated with preserved ecological process. They're places where humans have not had the chance to meddle, and ostensibly never will. In favoring wilderness preservation, wildlands are presented as vast repositories of natural resources to be preserved for inherent and scientific value. They are understood as strongholds of biodiversity, functioning systems that cleanse the atmosphere of excess carbon dioxide, and critical watersheds for downstream needs. They are valued natural laboratories, providing comparative baselines and standards for land health.

Yet does ecological inquiry really require that we set aside lands and manage them as absolute wilderness, devoid of human influence? Many argue that no, we do not. Opponents of wilderness say that ecological process can be studied and observed everywhere, and that it's next to impossible to accurately interpret any land as being wholly without human influence. However, proponents assert the value of what we have seen in preserved wilderness and what we can't see in human-altered lands elsewhere. The middle ground seems to come back to the fact that the science of ecology does not yet have all the answers, and that by not protecting wilderness in some form or quantity, we risk losing a critical component of our existence.

So we generally accept ecological process as a growing basis for ethical argument. Leopold's foresight is instructive:

The outstanding scientific discovery of the twentieth century is not television, or radio, but rather the complexity of the land organism. Only those who know the most about it can appreciate how little we know about it. The last word in ignorance is the man who says of an animal or plant: "What good is it?" If the land mechanism as a whole is good, then every part is good, whether we understand it or not. If the biota, in the course of aeons, has built something we like but do not understand, then who but a fool would discard seemingly useless parts? To keep every cog and wheel is the first precaution of intelligent tinkering.[7]

We must consider the potential knowledge wildlands hold; what we learn in the future may well depend on the wilderness resources we protect today. Wildlands present settings for possibility. Without them, the ability to be observers of the natural world as we know it is weakened, and our knowledge of ecology is forever biased and incomplete.

WILDERNESS WITHIN: CULTURAL CONNECTIONS

Wilderness provides a medium through which people can become reacquainted with the wildness within the human soul. Wallace Stegner writes in support of the Wilderness Act that "we simply need that wild country available to us, even if we never do more than drive to its edge and look in, for it can be a means of reassuring ourselves of our sanity as creatures, a part of the geography of hope."[8]

In his customarily irreverent style, Edward Abbey, the sharp-tongued spokesman for the deserts and canyons of the U.S. Southwest, expresses a similar sentiment and reminds us that wilderness is necessary to come to terms with our nomad spirit. "We need wilderness because we are wild animals," he writes in *The Journey Home.*

> Every man needs a place where he can go to go crazy in peace. Every Boy Scout troop deserves a forest to get lost, miserable and starving in. Even the maddest murderer of the sweetest wife should get the chance for a run to the sanctuary of the hills. If only for the sport of it. For the terror, freedom, and delirium. Because we need brutality and raw adventure, because men and women first learned to love in, under, and all around trees, because we need for every pair of feet and legs about ten leagues of naked nature, crags to leap from, mountains to measure by, deserts to finally die in when the heart fails.[9]

People traditionally lived more closely to the land than we do now. Humans have evolved with the influence of wildlands, and it's difficult to conjure up a vision of the human experience without this. Our efforts to preserve open space, create parklands within urban landscapes, set aside national parks, or retain the symbolism of wild creatures such as the bald eagle or bison is telling of the ongoing, integral relationship we have with the natural world. The influence of wilderness is apparent and inescapable. In our daily lives, we borrow images of forests and oceans, deserts and mountains. Calendars and kitchen trivets show beautiful scenes of wildflowers, stately trees, and majestic elk, and magazines and television commercials carry alluring images of wild places where we'd rather be. We discover a deeper connection while daydreaming at work about an upcoming river trip or smelling the scent of sage while driving down the interstate. As vicarious as this connection might become, we have never weakened the human manifest to have wild places and things as part of our condition.

STEWARDS OR CITIZENS?

Even among conservationists, a fundamental, philosophical schism exists with regard to the human relationship with wilderness. Are we meant to be stewards of the natural environment, as described in the book of Genesis, with "dominion over the fish of the sea, the birds of the air and the cattle, and over all the wild animals and all the creatures that crawl on the ground?"[10] Or are we just one species among the citizens of the world biotic community? The debate surrounding these questions is one of use, or conservation versus preservation, and has been going on since the beginning of this century, resurfacing in numerous forms.

The first publicized American dispute between these two schools of thought was the controversy in the early 1900s, in the wake of the catastrophic earthquake of 1906, over whether to dam California's Tuolumne River in Hetch Hetchy valley to provide San Francisco with more and better fresh water. Hetch Hetchy is said to have rivaled Yosemite in its natural splendor. Gifford Pinchot, patriarch of environmental stewards and first chief of the Forest Service, summarizes the utilitarian perspective in his well-known credo that the practice of conservation should serve "the greatest good, of the greatest number, for the longest run."[11] San Francisco needed the resource, and the Hetch Hetchy project would be a legitimate use of public lands to these ends. On the other hand, Pinchot's contemporary, the tenacious explorer and preservationist John Muir, felt that this spectacular valley should be preserved in its natural, wild state.

When Muir and Pinchot first met in 1896, they became friends. They had in common a strong desire to protect wildlands from wanton destruction. It soon became clear, however, that their fundamental loyalties were quite different. Pinchot was deeply committed to scientific management for human benefit, whereas Muir wanted to preserve wilderness for its own intrinsic and spiritual value. In the Hetch Hetchy debate, Muir referred to Pinchot and his followers as "temple destroyers, devotees of ravaging commercialism [who] seem to have a perfect contempt for Nature, and instead of lifting their eyes to the God of the Mountains, lift them to the Almighty Dollar."[12] In spite of the efforts of Muir and the Sierra Club, Congress voted in 1913 to build the dam in Hetch Hetchy, and today most of the valley lies under a large reservoir. The use versus preservation argument is still prevalent in the conservation movement, though it has become more complex as understanding and issues have evolved.

Historian Lynn White's 1967 article on the relationship between religion and the environment refocused attention on this schism. In this controversial article, White asserts that the Judeo-Christian tradition is largely responsible for western exploitation of nature. He contends that the origin of this responsibility is twofold. First, wilderness occurs in both the Old and New Testaments as a place of evil and asperity where people went for spiritual expurgation. (His critics point out that the Bible also contains references to wilderness and nature as sources of inspiration.) Second, the concept of stewardship places man above nature and other species.[13] Though the idea of stewardship does not directly foster a destructive attitude, it may promote a sense of separation between humans and the rest of the planet. White maintains that acceptance of the steward role places us in the position of benevolent dictator. Some consider the stewardship concept to be a stumbling block in arriving at a universally accepted ethic. For many ardent and committed conservationists, however, the philosophical debate is a distraction. The fact that we are able to decide what level of impact is acceptable automatically places us in a stewardship role.

The notion of the good steward prevails today in the management of U.S. public lands; all four federal land management agencies have philosophies grounded in the concept of benevolent, responsible stewardship for continued human use and enjoyment. Even the Wilderness Act, which is arguably a relatively nonanthropocentric piece of federal legislation, states that its purpose is "to secure for the American people of present and future generations the benefits of an enduring resource of wilderness . . . and these [lands] shall be administered for the use and enjoyment of the American people in such a manner as will leave them unimpaired for future use and enjoyment as wilderness."[14]

Though the foundation for a strong natural awareness has always been present within the Christian tradition, the environment has received little official attention from churches until recently. Church leaders and theologians—sometimes prompted by criticism from historians, environmentalists, and their congregations—are reevaluating the human relationship to the natural world and promoting a greater natural awareness. Father Thomas Berry, a Catholic monk, scholar, and director of the Riverdale Center for Religious Research in New York, represents a new breed of theologians searching for a spiritual orientation that returns us, in his words, "to our native place after a long absence, meeting once again with our kin in the earth community."[15]

Berry and others are drawing much of their inspiration from the wisdom of Native American cultures, which have foundations in their relationship with the natural world. An inspiring example of this relationship is expressed in an 1854 address attributed to Chief Sealth, or Seattle as he is now known, to a tribal assembly in the Pacific Northwest. The address marked the transfer of ancestral Indian lands to the U.S. government. Though documentation of the actual origin of the chief's address is scant, and it's known to contain several inconsistencies (he probably never saw a prairie or a buffalo),[16] it remains a poignant, powerful expression of a people's connectedness to the land.

> The Great Chief in Washington sends word that he wishes to buy our land. How can you buy or sell the sky, the warmth of the land? The idea is strange to us. If we do not own the freshness of the air and the sparkle of the water, how can you buy them . . . ?
>
> The shining water that moves in the streams and rivers is not just water but the blood of our ancestors. If we sell you our land you must remember that it is sacred, and you must teach your children that it is sacred, and that each ghostly reflection in the clear water of the lakes tells of events and memories in the life of my people. The water's murmur is the voice of my father's father. The rivers are our brother, they quench our thirst. I am a savage and do not understand any other way.

I have seen a thousand rotting buffalos on the prairie, left by the white man who shot them from a passing train. What is man without the beasts? If all the beasts were gone, men would die from a great loneliness of spirit. For whatever happens to the beasts, soon happens to man. All things are connected. Whatever befalls the earth, befalls the sons of the earth. If men spit upon the ground, they spit upon themselves. This we know.

The earth does not belong to man; man belongs to the earth. This we know. All things are connected like the blood that unites one family. Man did not weave the web of life; he is merely a strand in it. Whatever he does to the web, he does to himself.[17]

Contemporary philosophers, scientists, poets, and activists, many of whom are directly influenced by Native American cultures, are also espousing and advocating the idea that *Homo sapiens* is merely a citizen in a natural community of equals. This attitude is a departure from the stewardship concept and recognizes the intrinsic value of nonhuman species and natural processes. Muir, though himself the product of a strict Calvinist upbringing and heavily influenced by the likes of Emerson and Thoreau, was one of the first Americans to popularize this concept. Devall and Sessions have suggested that Muir's words and vision serve as inspiration for the deep ecology movement.[18] The following succinctly expresses Muir's idea of man's appropriate place in the natural order of things:

The world we are told was made for man. A presumption that is totally unsupported by facts. There is a very numerous class of men who are cast into painful fits of astonishment whenever they find anything, living or dead, in all God's universe, which they cannot eat or render in some way what they call useful to themselves. . . . Nature's object in making animals and plants might possibly be first of all the happiness of each one of them, not the creation of all for the happiness of one. Why ought man to value himself as more than an infinitely small composing unit of one great unit of creation? . . . The universe would be incomplete without the smallest transmicroscopic creature that dwells beyond our conceitful eyes and knowledge.[19]

The voice for nature grew louder throughout the twentieth century. In the 1930s and '40s, Leopold added ecological insight to Muir's spirituality, writing that "no important change in ethics was ever accomplished without an internal change in our intellectual emphasis, loyalties, affections and convictions. The proof that conservation has not yet touched these foundations of conduct lies in the fact that philosophy and religion have not yet heard of it."[20] Today, however, increasing numbers of philosophers, scientists, land managers, and religious leaders are contributing their voices and thoughts to the discourse about humans' relationship with the earth.

In 1954, natural history writer Joseph Wood Krutch explained that "the thing missing is love, some feeling for, as well as some understanding of, the inclusive community of rocks and soils, plants and animals, of which we are a part."[21] In the 1960s, environmentalism and wilderness preservation were put on the national agenda. At present, though we may still be far from possessing a national or international land ethic, Leopold would be

For some, wilderness areas seem almost like home. This can be a powerful tool in developing a wildlands ethic.

pleased to know that at least philosophy and religion have definitely heard of it. So the stewards versus citizens debate continues; both camps would preserve wild places, but for fundamentally different reasons.

WILDERNESS AS HOME

In 1964, Congress decreed that in designated Wilderness, humans (and their accoutrements) should be allowed only as visitors. The status of visitors seems to indicate a separation from wild places, and indeed, most trappings of modern civilization are incongruous with a wild setting.

Since the initial stirrings of the Wilderness Act, scholars, advocates, and policymakers have argued over the eligibility of lands to be included as Wilderness in the United States. Section 2(c) of the act states that wilderness is an area that is "untrammeled by man." *Untrammeled*, according to researchers John C. Hendee, George H. Stankey, and Robert C. Lucas, means "not subject to human controls and manipulations that hamper the free play of natural forces."[22] The act goes on to strengthen this by adding the condition of wilderness as lands that are "without permanent improvements or human habitation."

From the onset, these qualifying conditions have proved controversial. Supporters of Wilderness designation have argued that these strict definitions create too strong a condition of purity and unduly exclude lands that rightfully should be designated as Wilderness. Opponents state the contrary—that in following the letter of the law, many lands being considered for Wilderness designation simply do not qualify.

Though the act was signed into law, debate over its intent continues. Arguments can be made for natural conditions, but what does this mean? Where along the progression of dynamic natural process is the snapshot of naturalness taken? The lack of human influence or habitation can be a rallying point, but is this really a condition that wholly exists except in the most barren and inhospitable of lands? Environmental philosopher Mark Woods suggests that if the naturalness condition of wilderness is strictly past-oriented, then there can be no true wilderness, as finding land without the mark of human influence is nearly impossible. Instead, he proposes a "forward-looking" form of naturalness that "circumvents the problems raised by interpreting naturalness strictly in terms of the past" and is instead "conditioned by future possibilities as well as past causalities."[23] This definition of naturalness sees it as a condition of the present that does not necessarily exclude prior human influence; it incorporates the allowance of nature to have simply taken back the land under its own terms and by its own actions.

This form of naturalness proves fortuitous in considering wilderness as a past and perhaps present home. It allows one to consider stone walls from a reforested New England farmstead as part of the landscape and the remnants of Anasazi dwellings in a Utah canyon as congruous with a state of wilderness.

Allowing wilderness to be a place that was once home leads to examination of areas where humans still live in ways substantially dependent on wildlands. Often the development and evolution of a land ethic follows pathways of a pragmatic, and perhaps utilitarian, direction. In less affluent or less developed regions of the world, unmet demands for food and shelter make preservation of land a less attractive alternative and a more difficult option to ethically defend. Existence and survival are struggles that may allow a close relationship with wildlands, but the reality rarely affords the absolute preservation of them. With respect to agrarian and indigenous peoples, ethnobotanist Arturo Gomez-Pompa and anthropologist Andrea Kaus discuss this dilemma and propose that the "concept of wilderness as the untouched or untamed land is mostly an urban perception, the view of people who are far removed from the natural environment they depend on for raw resources." They explain that "indigenous groups in the tropics, for example, do not consider the tropical forest environment to be wild; it is their home."[24]

The fact that people live in and use areas that might otherwise be considered wild does not mean that these lands are not conserved or taken care of. A home is a place with which people grow greatly familiar, becoming accustomed to its physical features and temporal changes, its rhythms and needs. We learn how to maintain it, what it can provide us and, in turn, what we need to provide it to ensure its well-being. Such is the case for the peoples of many cultures, for whom wildlands are simply part of the fabric of their lives.

Perhaps the problem lies within the narrow definition of wilderness, which must recognize the possibility of self-interest in western thought and traditions. Our society has developed the idea that wilderness must be set aside and maintained in a state that is biased by our traditions. Our perception of wilderness is comfortably afforded us, colored by our unique economic, recreational, religious, scientific, and esthetic circumstances. Affluence has allowed us the time to form an exclusive relationship with wildlands and set aside certain lands to remain without human influence.

Does this dilute our familiar perception that "man himself is a visitor that must not remain"?[25] We must first remember to differentiate between closely defined and legally protected Wilderness Areas—where we have legislatively dictated that man does not remain—and other wilderness lands, where the subjectivity of our values holds sway. Then we must also muse on the meaning of home—the fact that a home need not be wood and concrete, but can be a collection of attributes and experiences, a familiar and comforting venue with which people feel an intrinsic relationship. Ultimately, we find that there are places where we should remain only visitors, and other lands where the contrary may be true. But home is simply where the heart is, and often this is in wilderness.

Our connections with wildlands are foundational in developing a personal ethic toward them. When we are in a place we feel is home, we are prone to act as residents. Good residents are good stewards and carry a strong ethic. We again find wisdom in the words of John Muir, who believed that wilderness is something people need, that "going to the mountains is going home."[26] The reflection of Dave Foreman, a pioneering and irascible scion of radical environmentalism, provides further affirmation: "I have spent many, many days and nights in wilderness areas from Alaska to Central America. I have not found that these landscapes where I am only a visitor separate me from Nature. When I am backpacking or canoeing, hunting or fishing in a Wilderness, I am home."[27]

3

Pioneers in Thought

Thousands of tired, nerve shaken, over-civilized people are beginning to find out that going to the mountains is going home; that wildness is a necessity; and that the mountain parks and reservations are useful not only as fountains of lumber and irrigating rivers, but as fountains of life.

—John Muir

"You are what you eat" is an oft-repeated phrase relating to personal appearance. Each person's ethics are shaped in a similar way by lifelong inputs of experience, education, and influence. A quote by Leopold or the words of Thoreau conjure up powerful stirrings that remind us of events or influences that are important to us. These influences become part of our mindset, validate our points of view, and give us cause to work toward a greater understanding of the world around us.

Pioneers in thought are among those who developed ideas and illustrated perceptions about nature and the natural world never before popularly advanced. Over the course of time, their words have become familiar. Their ideas have founded schools of thought. Their names have

THE WILDERNESS SOCIETY

Writer and wilderness advocate Aldo Leopold greatly influenced the development of wildlands policy in the twentieth century.

become synonymous with ecological vision and foresight. They brought forth wisdom that now guides us in seeking understanding of, good stewardship toward, and fruitful relationships with wildlands. They forged the path on which we now tread.

COMING TO TERMS WITH WILDERNESS

Wilder parts of the earthly landscape have affected art, literature, governments, philosophy, and religion for as long as those institutions have existed. Around the world, wildlands are revered and sought out as places for worship and enlightenment. For many eastern cultures, the high Himalayas are the abode of the gods. Mount Everest, or Sagamartha, as it is known to the Nepalese, is regarded by the indigenous people as the goddess of the universe. Among the gods of the people who settled in the high Andes of South America are the sun, moon, stars, and mountains. The poetry of Ralph Waldo Emerson and William Wordsworth and the paintings of Albert Bierstadt, George Catlin, and Thomas Moran were all inspired by the mountains, streams, wind, sunlight, and wildlife found beyond the edges of civilization.

Native American cultures incorporated a deep relationship with wilderness; western civilizations have not always shared the same reverence. Whether as a result of fear of and aversion to wild places, industrialization, increased urbanization, or the manifest destiny of growing nations, wilderness often became the victim of an increasing alienation between humans and the earth.[28] The destruction of wildlands was not unopposed, however. As early as the late eighteenth century, the Romantics—poets like Wordsworth and Lord Byron—lamented the loss of pristine lands. Later in America, transcendentalists challenged civilization's fear of wilderness and adulation of things tamed by mankind. Thoreau and Emerson were part of this movement, which sought to explore and define spirituality distinct from the Judeo-Christian traditions of European ascendancy. Thoreau's essay "Walking" captures the essence of his revolutionary defense of wilderness:

> I wish to speak a word for Nature, for absolute freedom and wildness, as contrasted with a freedom and culture merely civil—to regard man as

an inhabitant, or a part and parcel of Nature, rather than a member of society. . . .

In wildness is the preservation of the World. Every tree sends its fibers forth in search of the Wild. The cities import it at any price. Men plow and sail for it. From the forest and wilderness come the tonics and barks which brace mankind. Our ancestors were savages. The story of Romulus and Remus being suckled by a wolf is not a meaningless fable. The founders of every state which has risen to eminence have drawn their nourishment and vigor from a similar wild source. It was because the children of the Empire were not suckled by the wolf that they were conquered and displaced by the children of the northern forests who were. . . .

Life consists with wildness. The most alive is the wildest. Not yet subdued by man, its presence refreshes him. One who pressed forward incessantly and never rested from his labors, who grew fast and made infinite demands on life, would always find himself in a new country or wilderness, and surrounded by the raw material of life.[29]

Thoreau offered revolutionary thinking at a time when the national mindset was one of conquering, expanding, and developing. In *The Maine Woods*, Thoreau also reminds us of the need for a "base" connection with nature, one that we need to refresh, and that displays relevance in developing our ethic for wildlands:

The poet's, commonly, is not the logger's path, but a woodman's. . . . There are spirits . . . to whom no simplicity is barren. There are not only stately pines, but fragile flowers, like the orchises, commonly described as too delicate for cultivation, which derive their nutriment from the crudest mass of peat. These remind us, that, not only for strength, but for beauty, the poet must, from time to time, travel the logger's path and the Indian's trail, to drink at some new and more bracing fountain of the Muses, far in the recesses of the wilderness.[30]

Though their influence was scant during the day, Thoreau and his contemporaries were busy planting seeds of connectedness between man and nature. Emerson urged that nature's beauty and influence be a consideration in all of man's works. In an 1849 essay, he reflects on this connection: "In the wilderness, I find something more dear and connate than in streets or villages. In the tranquil landscape, and especially in the distant line of the horizon, man beholds somewhat as beautiful as his own nature."[31]

A DEVELOPING CONVICTION

Through the decades following the initial poetic and transcendentalist influence, the United States expanded in both population and land base. The Civil War challenged all to focus on healing the wounds of our still-young union. An American culture was forming, and it focused more on the tangible needs of the growing nation than on preservationist thought and influence. Nature offered challenges to robust development. It was not yet seen as an important element shaping the history of our culture or, as it was to become, a critical asset in retaining the health and wealth of the American experience and psyche. But there *were* those who recognized and chased its virtues. Some of these visionaries were simply following a personal passion and had the fortunate circumstance of gaining influence through well-heeled and politically influential associates. Others remained largely unnoticed during their time. Their work was to be remembered by future generations and at times when national priorities would allow for the luxury of wilderness.

George Perkins Marsh was one of those visionaries. Through life's experience, he gained an understanding of the relationship between society and nature, initially catalyzed in his native state of Vermont. Throughout the various careers he held—from sheep farmer to international diplomat—he observed, firsthand, global evidence of nature's demise at the hand of man. Marsh had visited and worked throughout Europe and the Middle East, where societies had profoundly changed natural landscapes through deforestation and desertification. At the time, this degradation of the land was generally attributed to natural manifestations or phenomena. Marsh saw differently, suggesting that human beings were the agents. He was the first to describe the interdependence of social and natural "landscapes," and in 1864, he issued his warnings in a book called *Man and Nature; or, Physical Geography as Modified by Human Action*. That humans could have a profound impact on the environment they lived in was an unconventional suggestion for the time, but Marsh's observations were duly noted and his predictions received favorably. Because of his work, practices in forestry worldwide were given much attention, and here in the United States, momentum began toward protection of our forested lands via establishment of reserves, eventually to become the national forest system. His influence on forestry practices has had lasting effects on our understanding and acceptance of humans' relationship with nature. For this he is often considered America's first environmentalist.

Though John Burroughs was seen during his time as a simple woodsman, he had a personal passion as naturalist and teacher, as well as an opportune association with the likes of John Muir and Theodore Roosevelt. His desire to preserve wilderness as part of the human condition and "open our eyes to the beauty of nature"[32] is illustrated in this excerpt from his 1877 work, *Birds and Poets:*

> There are those who look at Nature from the standpoint of conventional and artificial life,—from parlor windows and through gilt-edged poems,—the sentimentalists. At the other extreme are those who do not look at Nature at all, but are a grown part of her, and look away from her toward the other class,—the backwoodsman and pioneers, and all rude and simple persons. Then there are those in whom the two are united or merged,—the great poets and artists. In them the sentimentalist is corrected and cured, and the hairy and taciturn frontiersman has had experience to some purpose. The true poet knows more about Nature than the naturalists because he carries her open secrets in his heart.[33]

The latter part of the nineteenth century provided great opportunity to advance the relationship between Americans and what were now becoming public lands. As Marsh had predicted, the United States was beginning to see and feel the pinch of exploitation of natural resources. Wood was *the* resource needed to fuel the industrialization and growth of our nation, and forests were showing the effects of our uncontrolled hunger.

Developing modes of transportation, particularly the railroads, allowed Americans to observe the natural wonders of the continent for themselves, and as an alarming side note, they witnessed the effects of rampant growth.

Now entering the dialogue was Scotsman John Muir, an influential wilderness wanderer who, as fortune would have it, ended up finding a true home in the Sierras of California. His name is inseparable from Yosemite Valley; the Sierra Club, which he founded; and the landmark battle to save Hetch Hetchy valley. His image remains as that of consummate adventurer, passionate naturalist, and primary player in the dawn of wilderness advocacy.

In Muir's time, conservation—generally seen as prudent use—of public land and resources was being adopted as the order of the day. Muir had a personal vision that went beyond the allowances of the conservation mindset. His concern was both for the spiritual nature of man and for nature itself. The promise of safeguarding these could be assured only through preservation. His reverence for nature is well understood in this urging: "Climb the mountains and get their good tidings. Nature's peace will flow into you as sunshine flows into trees. The winds will blow their own freshness into you, and the storms their energy, while cares will drop off like autumn leaves."[34]

Muir was an astute observer of the workings of nature, a pioneer in the stirrings of ecological insight. His simple observation that "when we try to pick out anything by itself, we find it hitched to everything else in the Universe,"[35] illustrates the synergy he had with the natural world. Muir was an advocate for his preservationist ideals. He had learned that protection of lands he held dear could be initiated by sharing his insights, knowledge, and feelings, but that tenacious action would be necessary to affect the political winds of the day. In the following passage, he couples absolute respect for the forests he knew so well with the resigned understanding that their fate is in uncertain hands:

> Any fool can destroy trees. They cannot run away; and if they could, they would still be destroyed,— chased and hunted down as long as fun or a dollar could be got out of their bark hides, branching horns, or magnificent bole backbones. Few that fell trees plant them; nor would planting avail much towards getting back anything like the noble primeval forests. During a man's life only saplings can be grown, in the place of the old trees—tens of centuries old—that have been destroyed. It took more than three thousand years to make some of the trees in these Western woods,—trees that are still standing in perfect strength and beauty, waving and singing in the mighty forests of the Sierra. Through all the wonderful, eventful centuries since Christ's time—and long before that—God has cared for these trees, saved them from drought, disease, avalanches, and a thousand straining, leveling tempests and floods; but he cannot save them from fools, only Uncle Sam can do that.[36]

Muir's efforts and strong convictions found audience all the way to the highest office in the land. He proved influential in the founding of the country's first national parks, including his beloved Yosemite. Theodore Roosevelt's conservation initiatives were greatly influenced by Muir, and his administration accomplished the initial founding of several national parks, began a system of national monuments, and set aside great amounts of land, later to be incorporated into the national forest system. During this time, the battle to save Hetch Hetchy valley was engaged. Even though this fight was lost, Muir's legacy was strengthened. Today he is held as an exemplary model of what conviction and determination can accomplish for the preservation of wilderness.

In the decades that followed, the conservation movement continued its advance into the governance of public lands. The federal government found itself confronted with the challenges of managing vast tracts of land that were increasingly valued by U.S. citizens. On one hand, the "greatest good" called for a proper scheme for their conservation—again, not excluding exploitation. On the other, the loss of natural values was no longer going unnoticed. Whatever the ultimate disposition of public lands, a vision for their future had begun to form, and their stewardship was manifest upon the government.

Under Roosevelt's administration, Gifford Pinchot rose to prominence as the first chief of the Division of Forestry. Scientific management became the calling of the day. This shift engaged the prevention of reckless exploitation and also promulgated the need to manage public lands for future needs. The federal government's role as active steward was strengthened. But within this stewardship there was little movement toward the preservationist goal of absolute protection for intrinsic worth.

In the 1920s and '30s, Robert Marshall, well educated in forestry and its terms of economic management, added important insight. Despite a strong academic foundation, Marshall was most influenced by his active wanderings and long-distance treks among the wild, roadless areas of North America. He believed these expanses to be critical to those of a similar bent. "For me, and for thousands with similar inclinations," he writes, "the most important passion of life is the overpowering desire to escape periodically from the clutches of a mechanistic civilization. To us the enjoyment of solitude, complete independence, and the beauty of undefiled panoramas is absolutely essential to happiness."[37]

In 1935, Marshall's beliefs found fruition through the Wilderness Society, of which he was one of the principal founders. His expression of these beliefs reflected his zeal and pointed toward the lasting influence he was to have on the valuation and preservation of wildlands: "The preservation of a few samples of undeveloped territory is one of the most clamant issues before us today. Just a few more years of hesitation and the only trace of that wilderness which has exerted such a fundamental influence in molding American character will lie in the musty pages of pioneer books. . . . To avoid this catastrophe demands immediate action."[38]

The bias of history often passes over major contributions to the development of the conservation movement. Some of the most profound stirrings of the movement came from women, including Florence Merriam Bailey, Rosalie Barrow Edge, and Marjory Stoneman Douglas. In the late 1800s, many burgeoning naturalists had developed interests in the bird life of this continent. Birds are among the most available, visible, and attractive examples of wildlife, and people with a leaning toward studying the natural world are quickly drawn to them. Such was the case with both Bailey and Edge.

Florence Merriam Bailey, a prolific writer and exemplary naturalist of the late 1800s and early 1900s, had a passion for studying live birds. She disdained the practice of the day that required killing them for study in collections and to satisfy the fashion industry's demand for their feathers. Her numerous books and journal articles focused on the protection of birds and did much to reduce both of these practices, ultimately resulting in Congress banning the interstate shipping of birds. Today, Bailey is recognized as an astute naturalist. Her influence on the conservation movement came out of educating the public about the natural history and value of birds. The growing conservation movement enjoyed great support and gained direction from her followers.

Rosalie Barrow Edge was born in 1877 into prominence and wealth. Events in her life led her to passionately pursue bringing equal rights to women—and to become a serious birder. She had her greatest influence by championing reform of the National Association of Audubon Societies, whose directors in the 1920s and early 1930s had fallen into collusion with commercial wildlife harvesters and remained indifferent to a growing ecological consciousness that eschewed such activities as the sport hunting of hawks. She used her activist clout to help reform the society, and when they refused to support her efforts to create a wildlife sanctuary at Hawk Mountain, Pennsylvania, she undertook to do so herself. It remains today, a haven along the migratory pathways for eagles, falcons, and hawks.

Marjory Stoneman Douglas, well known as the "Defender of the Everglades," began her trade as a writer and journalist in Miami in 1915. Long before conservation became a popularized notion, she took on its cause and undertook a mission that would last the majority of her long life of 108 years. Her cause was the preservation of the Everglades, a unique ecosystem critically dependent on its wetlands and water sources. Douglas fought the encroachment of agriculture and development that, with the aid of the Army Corps of Engineers, was steadily destroying the very sources of water that create this magnificent wetland. Her tireless work, begun well before scientists recognized the magnitude of threats to this region, led to today's ongoing efforts to restore and protect the Everglades. Douglas knew the magnitude of her fight and remained committed to it. Her words identify a mission for conservationists forevermore: "The most unhappy thing about conservation is that it is never permanent. If we save a priceless woodland today, it is threatened from another quarter tomorrow."[39]

Quiet yet critical contributions came from within the land management agencies themselves. Arthur Carhart was a landscape architect charged with the task of surveying a road around Trappers Lake in the White River National Forest, with a view toward homesites on the lakeshore. His resultant recommendation was that no development be permitted; in essence, the best use of the land was to leave it alone. Surprisingly, his suggestion was endorsed, and Trappers Lake remains roadless and undeveloped to this day. This designation marked the first application of the wilderness preservation concept in Forest Service history,[40] and has had great effect on the development of preservationist ideals, including those of Leopold.

Aldo Leopold became a visionary as a simple extension of his life's passion. Through observation and study he was driven toward an understanding of nature. Through various posts in federal agencies and academic work at the University of Wisconsin, he focused on enacting land management policies that were based on sound scientific information. During the 1920s and '30s, this impetus was greatly needed, as fledgling agencies were busy developing direction for the lands they oversaw but had only a rudimentary understanding of how the policies enacted affected the lands they targeted. Leopold observed the intricacies of natural systems and the interconnectedness that was primary to their functioning and health. His work both explored and strongly promoted these ideas, catalyzing the field of ecology and creating initial momentum for the field of wildlife conservation. The respect he gained from the scientific and management communities enabled him to promote ideas for the establishment of natural areas within national forests. He opened the debate surrounding the idea of wilderness and rallied support for it. In 1924, his beliefs and work yielded landmark results when the first official wilderness area, the Gila Wilderness Area in New Mexico, was created.

Leopold was a greatly successful influence on natural resource policy in this country. But he is perhaps even more widely remembered as an essayist who had the remarkable ability to understand and pursue science and land management, and mold it into a "land ethic," expressed in his timeless *Sand County Almanac:* "The land ethic simply enlarges the boundaries of the community to include soils, waters, plants, and animals, or collectively: the land. . . . A land ethic of course cannot prevent the alteration, management, and use of these 'resources,' but it does affirm their right to continued existence, and, at least in spots, their continued existence in a natural state."[41]

Leopold's astute understanding of the relationships within the natural world encouraged all people to examine their place within it. Through his influence, beliefs and loosely founded convictions began to come together as a set of values employing scientific basis and understanding.

In the decades of the mid-twentieth century, the United States' scheme for land management advanced and formed within the Departments of Interior (National Park Service, Bureau of Land Management, U.S. Fish and Wildlife Service) and Agriculture (USDA Forest Service). The perceived crown jewels of public lands were protected as showpieces under the National Park System. The Bureau of Land Management (BLM) was authorized to oversee grazing lands and other holdings of unknown (and as it turns out, underestimated) value. The Forest Service, whose initial role revolved around the resources of timber and water, grew expansively in size. It began to feel pressure from a public with a diversity of views on what constitutes a valuable resource and how we as a nation should spend or protect ours. The United States was reaping great benefits from nature's tidings, but the real cost of industrialization, growth, and economic power was a shrinking unexploited land base.

The automobile allowed people to travel more, experience the land firsthand, and understand the finite quantity of wilderness. This was the same wilderness that, a century or so before, had been seen as an obstacle to development—a place to be feared, tamed, and conquered. The years following World War II saw both an economic surge and a baby boom. Americans had passed the tough times of the last few decades—war, the Great Depression, and the Dust Bowl—and the United States was solidly on its way to being the dominant global force. In terms of wildlands, some administrative wheels were in motion. The government had begun to set aside primitive areas within national forests and had designated national parks, in large part "to conserve the scenery and the natural and historic objects and the wild life therein."[42] Outdoor recreation was beginning to boom. Smokey the Bear and Bambi—symbols that brought recognition of our responsibility and indebtedness toward wild nature and asked us to accept responsibility for our actions—had made their way into the public spotlight. The nation's political and economic climate still encouraged development and resource-extractive industries, but it was now filled with vocal and active challenges delivered by citizens empowered with knowledge, vision, and passion.

The Sierra Club and the Wilderness Society were growing in membership. They and similar organizations proved increasingly valuable in gathering like-minded influence and affecting public land management and policy. Exemplifying the drive of these organizations were two persistent leaders in the effort to protect wilderness: David Brower and Howard Zahniser. Brower, an early member and later the first executive director of the Sierra Club, fought tirelessly for the preservation and responsible use of wilderness. He was profoundly influential in the creation of several national parks and in the establishment of the National Wilderness Preservation System. When Dinosaur National Monument and, later, the Grand Canyon were threatened by dams, Brower led—and won—the fight for their protection. His tenacious efforts spurred the American environmental movement onto new battlegrounds and gave it a momentum and strength of numbers that made it a force to be reckoned with for years to come.

Zahniser served as executive secretary of the Wilderness Society, following in the philosophical footsteps of Robert Marshall. He too was a formidable force, battling through decades of the formative years of the National Wilderness Preservation System. In 1956, he helped introduce the first Wilderness Act into Congress, and in the following years, he wrote sixty-six drafts, seeing it through eighteen congressional hearings. The act was finally passed and signed into law on September 3, 1964—an event that created a lasting legacy of Wilderness in this country and formally served notice of the significant place that wildlands held in American society and culture.

The United States was obliged to function with the input of its citizens. Nature was becoming a well-known and valued element of the American psyche. The protection and preservation of land as wilderness was championed by growing numbers of people who cared about the future condition of their country. The nation's land ethic was emerging.

EMBRACING WILDERNESS

Wilderness played an important role in Leopold's land ethic, not only as the realm of healthy ecological processes, but also as a reminder to humans of our relationship with the natural world, a relationship from which we are overinsulated by the comforts of society. "Your true modern," wrote Leopold, "is separated from the land by many middlemen and by innumerable physical gadgets. He has no vital relation to it; to him it is the space between cities on which crops grow. Turn him loose for a day on the land, and if the spot does not happen to be a golf links or a scenic area, he is bored stiff."[43]

Wildlands are fundamental to the human condition; they do more than just provide a connection between people and nature. They are the raw material of human culture, according to Leopold, and "give definition and meaning to the human enterprise." Nature provides the "single starting-point, to which man returns again and again to organize yet another search for a durable scale of values."[44]

Roderick Nash, a historian of human thought and ideas at the University of California–Santa Barbara, says that original culture did not begin in the United States until artists and writers began deriving their inspiration from wilderness rather than from their European predecessors. Wilderness, he says, is a source of cultural distinction and independence in this country.[45] Wallace Stegner, novelist and historian, articulated the American cultural debt to wilderness when he wrote that "an American, insofar as he is new and different at all, is a civilized man who has renewed himself in the wild."[46] There exists a clear relationship for Americans between wilderness and freedom. The wild frontier symbolized freedom from the restraints and confines of civilization.

Sigurd Olson, an exceptional writer, leading conservationist, and academician during the formative years of wilderness preservation, helped shape the national debate about the meaning of wilderness. His words still help form our national consciousness, remind us of our intrinsic needs, and consider what we must protect to save ourselves:

> In some men, the need of unbroken country, primitive conditions and intimate contact with the earth is a deeply rooted cancer gnawing forever at the illusion of contentment with things as they are. For months or years this hidden longing may go unnoticed and then, without warning, flare forth in an all consuming passion that will not bear denial. Perhaps it is the passing of a flock of wild geese in the spring, perhaps the sound of

running water, or the smell of thawing earth that brings the transformation. Whatever it is, the need is more than can be borne with fortitude, and for the good of their families and friends, and their own particular restless souls they head toward the last frontiers and escape.[47]

These pioneers in thought have lent us much in societal and cultural gain. Their words transcended the bounds of politics, economics, the arts, and social science, influencing the future by exploring new ground. They helped us recognize and accept the virtues of nature, reminded us that we do not stand apart from the ground we tread, and saw to it that a wild legacy would be a real and lasting part of this nation. Their work guaranteed that we, and those who follow, will retain the fundamental human ability to exercise the wildness within our souls, and that the natural character of many great parts of this country—indeed, this earth—will be neither lost nor forgotten.

4

Current Perspectives

We must ask ourselves as Americans, "Can we really survive the worship of our own destructiveness?" We do not exist in isolation. Our sense of community and compassionate intelligence must be extended to all life forms, plants, animals, rocks, rivers, and human beings. This is the story of our past and it will be the story of our future.

—Terry Tempest Williams

Wilderness itself is the basis of all our civilization. I wonder if we have enough reverence for life to concede to wilderness the right to live on?

—Margaret Murie

Exploitation of resources and loss of natural values have always been contentious issues, but the signing into law of the Wilderness Act, the growth of environmental understanding, and an increasingly engaged public give cause for optimism. Before the act, new attitudes and the actions of people toward wilderness and conservation were critical in the evolution of a national consciousness. These now play out as key elements in our political and land-management framework. As current issues and challenges to the environment and wildlands arise, ethics catalyze our actions and help us set a course that respects the values and relationships that humans share with nature.

When viewed from a societal rather than individual perspective, ethics become a sort of lofty peer pressure, an accepted code of conduct based on conventional morality. The notion that this ought to include relationships between humans and nature is a relatively new concept in Western philosophy. It is a tribute to Leopold that the wisdom he advanced in his day still stands as a foundational primer explaining humans' connection with nature.

Leopold's "The Land Ethic" defines an ethic and discusses the expansion of ethical boundaries:

> This extension of ethics, so far studied only by philosophers, is actually a process in ecological evolution. Its sequences may be described in ecological as well as in philosophical terms. An ethic, ecologically, is a limitation on freedom of action in the struggle for existence. An ethic, philosophically, is a differentiation of social from anti-social conduct. These are two definitions of one thing. The thing has its origin in the tendency of interdependent individuals or groups to evolve modes of cooperation. The ecologist calls these symbioses. Politics and economics are advanced symbioses in which the original free-for-all competition has been replaced, in part, by co-operative mechanisms with an ethical content. . . . Ethics are possibly a kind of community instinct in-the-making.[48]

Roderick Nash discusses this progression in *The Rights of Nature,* which presents an expanding umbrella of ethical awareness and behavior from the preethical past to a hypothetical future. The umbrella initially encompasses only pure self-interest and gradually opens up to include family, tribe, community, nation, and ultimately (and perhaps hypothetically) nonhuman life and nonliving matter. Legislation in a democracy is to some extent a reflection of social attitudes. English and American legislation that gradually extended rights to oppressed segments of society, such as women, African Americans, and Native Americans, correlates to Nash's opening umbrella. The Endangered Species Act of 1973, which legislates a right of existence for all nonhuman species, was regarded by Nash as an indication of movement toward the outer limits of the ethical circle.

Two philosophies that support Nash's concept are deep ecology and bioregionalism. The two basic principles of deep ecology, as developed by Norwegian philosopher Arne Naess, are self-realization and biocentric equality. The principle of biocentric equality states that every component of the biosphere, as part of the interrelated whole, has its own intrinsic value and thus an equal right to pursue its own self-realization, or personal potential. But Naess discards the assumption that humans and other beings of any kind exist independently of one another. He asserts that narrowly defining the individual self encourages separation and isolation from one another and from the land.[49] When people lack feelings of connection with something, they are more likely to abuse it. Naess instead expands the definition of self along the Hindu notion that the "Self abides in all beings and all beings in Self."[50] This leads toward a universal altruism, wherein individuals will identify more closely with the good of the whole.

Differences between deep ecology and bioregionalism are subtle. Bioregionalism is an outgrowth of the American counterculture of the 1960s and derives much of its wisdom from Native American traditions. The movement of bioregionalism recognizes that the current political divisions that societies have created bear little relationship to geographic areas, which share geophysical and biological components such as soils, climate, watershed, flora and fauna, as well as a unique cultural geography. If societies were to reorganize by bioregions, people would have a commonality of place, better grasp how to live in that place, and likely form a much stronger ethical connection with it.

The tenets of deep ecology extend far beyond common understanding of the word *ecology* and attempt to redefine our philosophical and religious worldview. Naess first coined the term "deep ecology" in 1973 while trying to describe the "deeper, more spiritual approach to nature exemplified in the writings of Aldo Leopold and Rachel Carson."[51] Devall and Sessions, coauthors of *Deep Ecology: Living as if Nature Mattered,* are largely responsible for advancing the term in this country.

Most conservationists and environmental organizations have ideals in common with deep ecologists and bioregionalists, but many of them also embrace a more pragmatic or practical approach to conservation. While for some the differences represent a philosophical schism, for others they are the result of compromises made in the context of the political process in order to get results.

Although a land ethic as described by Aldo Leopold still provokes argument, it is an idea seen by growing numbers as a necessary and logical evolution. Proponents of such an ethic are found in a broad spectrum of philosophical and political ideologies, and they do not always agree with one another. Local and regional grassroots conservation organizations and land trusts exist all over the country and attract large memberships. These organizations present a wide range of approaches in advancing their missions; it is illustrative to examine a few of them.

Near one end of the spectrum is the Izaak Walton League, an organization composed largely of traditional outdoor recreationists, such as hunters and anglers. The league has promoted responsible backcountry behavior since its inception in 1922, and it established an outdoor ethics program in 1977 to further that goal. Near the other, more radical end of the spectrum are Earth First!—an activist organization notorious for its "monkey-wrenching"—and the Earth Liberation Front (ELF), which, tossing aside current legal bounds and process, encourages and instigates destructive and sometimes catastrophic means to achieve its anarchistic ends. Large conservation organizations such as the Wilderness Society and Sierra Club fall somewhere in between. They promote stewardship of wild places, but according to more radical preservationists, they make too many compromises along the way. The Natural Resources Defense Council advances its ground by tenaciously working within the legal mechanism. The Nature Conservancy circumvents the lengthy process of changing societal norms and political ideology by operating within them, purchasing parcels of land to meet its preservation goals. Extolling the absolute and inarguable rights of nature lends momentum to groups such as Greenpeace and People for the Ethical Treatment of Animals (PETA), which advance their messages through media and other popular channels along with direct, visible, and often controversial actions in efforts to raise public awareness and confront issues immediately, when time and deliberation are not deemed affordable.

ENVIRONMENTAL ETHICS

The field of environmental ethics harbors the genre of philosophical discussion that examines the relationship between humans and all of the elements our environment comprises. This can include all forms of life—animals, plants, microorganisms—as well as nonliving features such as rocks, water, and air. Within this framework, consideration is also given to ecological concepts such as dynamic natural process, the functioning of ecosystems, and the interconnectedness of constituent pieces of nature. The field of environmental ethics lends itself capably to the study of issues affecting wilderness and gives insight in situations where decisions of right and wrong must be made.

As people learn that we are ecologically interdependent with our environment, we seek to protect our habitat. Occasionally important events catalyze these shifts. Perhaps no contribution was as far reaching in opening people's eyes as Rachel Carson's. In her 1962 landmark book, *Silent Spring*, Carson, a marine biologist and zoologist, provided an exposé of the chemical and pesticide industry and the damage, largely unknown at the time, that it was inflicting on the environment and the country's water supply. Her work aroused the environmental consciousness of millions of Americans and lent scientific basis to the environmental movement, in a way akin to the influence of Leopold. Carson's revelations fueled active self-examination that sparked development within the field of environmental ethics. Her warnings remain good counsel today, as exemplified by this excerpt from

DEBORAH SUSSEX

One of the more controversial questions in environmental ethics is whether animals and even plant life can be said to have rights.

her 1951 work, *The Sea around Us*: "It is a curious situation that the sea, from which life first arose should now be threatened by the activities of one form of that life. But the sea, though changed in a sinister way, will continue to exist; the threat is rather to life itself."[52]

Recognition that humans are connected to the world we live in has challenged us to seek answers to important questions: Should we recognize this connection with nature and not simply dominate it? Should we aspire to be beneficent, extracting resources we need from the earth, but giving back to it in equally helpful ways? What good is it to enhance *our* existence while destroying the very things we need to survive? Does the natural world have rights that should be considered as we advance in our dominion over the planet? Following Carson's revelations, the general public would no longer casually accept the promises of technological science without scrutinizing the effects it would have on our health and that of the natural world.

VALUE SYSTEMS

The realm of environmental ethics must address human virtues, needs, and survival, but it also must consider the same for the natural world. How to assess and place value on these is a source of much discussion among philosophers. Theories of value initiate many ethical debates. Assessing the worth of organisms, ecosystems, and the environment is an essential step in ethical consideration.

Ethical theories support the idea that all living organisms have inherent worth. Because of this, they are recognized with undeniable and intrinsic value, a sort of status on the scale of ethical economy. *Individualist* schools of thought present the individual organism as the only probable unit of true ethical worth. On the other hand, *holistic* views value the individual, but only as much as or less than the well-being of the ecological community as a whole.

The value of an organism is altered by characteristics. An individual, living organism that feels pleasure and pain, sensations experienced only through self-awareness and subjective ability, is given more value than an organism that does not experience these.[53] An organism that is sentient—capable of feeling and perceiving—has a greater connection with its environment, and a value that arguably increases with its complexity. The nonsentient elements of the natural world are organisms such as plants and single-celled and very primitive animals. Along with rocks and other nonliving features of the environment, they are generally given little or no ethical value. Individualistic approaches to ethics place individual, living organisms at the apex of ethical consideration, creating troubling arguments for those who find natural processes and the life-and-death dynamics of nature of greater importance.

Holistic ethical thinking considers whether it is more appropriate to place a higher value on a collection of individuals such as a population, species, or even an ecosystem, which contains many interconnected organisms and forms of life. Individualists counter that these collections cannot possess the sensations or sentience of an individual organism and therefore cannot be given ethical value. Holistic viewpoints maintain that value also resides in ecological wholes—functioning communities complete in

James Lovelock's Gaia hypothesis treats all life on the planet as interdependent parts of a single organism.

all their parts—and generally make for a more accommodating stance in discussions of entire natural systems.
These theories have made steady inroads into the management of natural resources and are proving influential.

On the radical end of holistic theory is an idea pursued by James Lovelock, the Gaia hypothesis. Lovelock's
pursuits were in science, with a particular bent toward
recognizing and identifying the base determinants of
planetary life. Through his work, the idea of the earth
behaving as a single living organism evolved. This "super
organism," Gaia, has survived many crises and is clearly
capable of adapting to ever-changing conditions. The elements critical to Gaia's survival are its "vital organs,"
those simple organisms such as bacteria and single-celled
marine algae that produce the primary requisites of
higher life forms. Higher organisms that depend on the
successful functioning of Gaia would be prioritized as
expendable relative to the well-being of the planet.
Humans, therefore, have a self-interested duty to avoid
actions harmful to the equilibrium in which Gaia exists,
as these disruptions might mean the end of human life.
The planet is the supreme concern; we are passengers that
must mind our behavior.[54] The Gaia hypothesis was, and
still is, rejected by many, especially evolutionary biolo-
gists. But it advances an intriguing framework for holistic
environmental thought and provides a fitting bandwagon
for more radical elements of the environmental movement—such as Earth First!—that operate with staunch
biocentric goals.

In order to make decisions and take action when
wrestling with the complex nature of resource management, conciliatory approaches become important. Philosopher and environmental ethicist Holmes Rolston
represents a key position that allows for both individual

and holistic values in the natural world. Rolston accepts that characteristics of individuals have value, but he goes on to explain that value at the species level comes from the genetic sets that define a species—in essence, a sort of property commonly shared by both species and the individual, where it is expressed. Rolston considers the ecosystem as a life-creating process, an interconnected matrix within which life evolved and continues to develop and, as such, an appropriate unit for moral concern.[55]

Enhancing the discussion is ecofeminism, a recently developing branch of environmental ethics that seeks to emphasize relationships between humans and nature. Ecofeminism explores particular worldviews, contexts of human experience and location, and emotional elements in the construction of ethical theory. Accepting the uniqueness and variety in human experience, environmental ethicist Val Plumwood explains that ethical reasoning should "find a form which encourages sensitivity to the conditions under which we exist on the earth . . . and enable us to acknowledge our debt to the sustaining others of the earth."[56] Relationships become a critical element in fundamentally defining an individual. This approach is very useful in that it recognizes and accepts a dynamic world and the complex nature of ecosystems.

Environmental ethics and value systems present a rich diversity of discussion and thought; however, some of their internal disagreements run the risk of eternal argument. There is an increasing need and desire to answer environmental questions and foster management action without the theoretical wiggle room afforded by open-ended philosophical discourse. To address today's issues, applicable elements from all schools of thought are generally taken into account in addressing the profound complexities and greatly varying contexts of ethical decision making and environmental challenges. However, this approach must accede to the fact that action sometimes results only through compromise, a principle well known in democracy.

THE RIGHTS OF NATURE

A broad anthropocentric approach to environmental values forms the underpinnings of most current environmental policy. One of the greatest contributions of environmental ethics is its influence in changing this momentum, contesting the anthropocentric valuation of the world. New ways of thinking are encroaching on traditional mindsets, as the field of environmental ethics and the political, legal, and economic worlds of resource management come together.

Environmentalists have frequently engaged the courts in attempts to establish or enforce rights for nature and wilderness. Christopher Stone's revolutionary 1972 essay, *Should Trees Have Standing?* proposed legal rights for natural objects other than humans. Stone, a professor of legal philosophy at the University of Southern California, adds a legal perspective to Leopold's extension of ethics. He cites legal case history that documents the gradual extension of rights in the United States to women, children, and minorities, and then goes on to propose that "we give legal rights to forests, oceans, rivers and other so-called 'natural objects' in the environment—indeed, to the natural environment as a whole."[57] This essay was an important step in opening Roderick Nash's ethical umbrella.

Stone wrote his essay in an attempt to influence the 1972 Sierra Club versus Morton Supreme Court decision, in which the highest court upheld an earlier opinion that the Sierra Club had no legal standing to bring the case to court. The Sierra Club had filed a complaint on behalf of

Mineral King Valley, a wilderness area in the Sierra Nevada, when the Forest Service granted a permit to Walt Disney Enterprises to develop a $35 million resort complex in the valley. Although the court found that the Sierra Club did not have sufficient stake in the outcome to bring the matter to trial, it did offer advice about how the group might effectively demonstrate standing in future cases. In his dissenting opinion, Justice William O. Douglas provides the most enlightening and encouraging words:

> Inanimate objects are sometimes parties in litigation. . . . So it should be as respects valleys, alpine meadows, rivers, lakes, estuaries, beaches, ridges, groves of trees, swampland, or even air that feels the destructive pressures of modern technology and modern life. The river, for example, is the living symbol of all the life it sustains or nourishes— fish, aquatic insects, water ouzels, otter, fisher, deer, elk, bear, and all other animals, including man, who are dependent on it or who enjoy it for its sight, its sound, or its life. The river as plaintiff speaks for the ecological unit of life that is part of it. Those people who have a meaningful relation to that body of water—whether it be a fisherman, a canoeist, a zoologist, or a logger—must be able to speak for the values which the river represents and which are threatened with destruction.[58]

Today people argue the value of natural fire regimes or complete and functioning ecosystems, find worth in clean air and watersheds, and express the inherent value of wilderness unfettered by mechanized devices. Philosophical discussions have led to some innovative and

DEBORAH SUSSEX

It's easy to see why the popular arts find inspiration in the beauty of wild places.

important leaps in our nation's system of legal justice. Environmental ethics invites us to consider the value of an organism, ecosystem, or natural process. It allows us to more fully frame the consequences of our actions upon these things and chart a course that more fairly integrates their values with ours.

SOURCES OF INFLUENCE

Philosophers are busy sowing the seeds of influence in ethics, and their work freely circulates among their philosophical and academic brethren. The worlds of politics, land management, ecology, wildland recreation, and other pursuits receive great enrichment from this discourse. The evolution and development of ethical insight is fostered by varied and active channels of communication.

The fields of popular literature and the visual arts have been perhaps the greatest contributors to date in influencing wildland ethics. The writings of Thoreau, Emerson, Leopold, and Carson are well known. Currently a strong, immensely talented, and growing cadre of writers brings nature's wisdom and prose into our lives. Authors such as Barry Lopez, Wallace Stegner, and Richard Nelson offer vivid reflections of nature. The poetic interpretation of Gary Snyder draws us back to the teachings of and unifies our partnership with nature. And who can say that they haven't been influenced, in one way or another, by the rallying urgings of Edward Abbey or the wisdom of the Lorax, via Theodore Geisel's Dr. Seuss? Terry Tempest Williams reminds us of what we gain from wild places and how the human experience cannot be full without them: "To be whole. To be complete. Wildness reminds us what it means to be human, what we are connected to rather than what we are separate from."[59]

Visual arts continually connect us with the natural world. Ansel Adams's timeless images, like the earlier paintings of Thomas Moran, Albert Bierstadt, and George Catlin, unveiled for us the wonders of this land. Today the works of leagues of artists and photographers shape our ties with the wild and strengthen the human incentive to serve as good stewards.

Great naturalists such as Ann Zwinger and Frank Craighead have had tremendous influence in bringing people in touch with nature. The lives of Olaus and Mardie Murie were driven by the need to explore and understand the natural world. They not only studied and taught us about nature, but also delivererd a passionate message about protecting the wild places they loved.

Researcher, naturalist, and author Edward O. Wilson enhances our understanding of nature by interpreting the discoveries of science. These are the explainers of our time, who have never lost sight of the importance of the full community of life. These exemplary people have made it their life's work to give us a greater understanding of the relationships we have with wildlands and wild creatures. They have shown us that the natural world matters and instilled within us a lasting sense of unity with it and responsibility for its care.

Though the teachings of literature, art, and philosophy have their virtues, a true bond with and understanding of nature requires that we spend time there. The great scholars, academicians, artists, philosophers, and teachers all have. As devotees, enthusiasts, students, and friends of wildlands, so must we. Professional mountain guide and philosopher Jack Turner explains a need for direct experience in wilderness in order to achieve a "personalizing of nature." He argues that in order to perpetuate a "phenology," a transferable knowledge of nature's relationships and rhythms, akin to those of Thoreau and Leopold, we must establish residency—have direct experience—in wild nature. We cannot effectively learn about nature from "mere concepts and abstractions . . . because that which needs to be shared is beyond concepts and abstractions."

> To be absorbed in this life is to merge with larger patterns. Here ecology is not studied but felt. You know these truths the way you know hot from cold; they are immune from doubt and argument. Here is the intimate knowledge conservation biology often seeks to rediscover, the common wisdom of primary peoples.

So we are left with the vital importance of residency in wild nature, and a visceral knowledge of that wildness, as the most practical means of preserving the wild. What we need now is a new tradition of the wild that teaches us how human beings live best by living in and studying the wild without destroying it.

In short it is a tradition that could again compel respect, care and love for wild nature in a way that philosophical foundations, aesthetics, moral theory, and politics cannot compel. It is a tradition we need to recreate for ourselves . . . a wild tradition of our own.[60]

WILDERNESS VALUES

What exactly are the virtues of wilderness addressed by wildland ethics? For most, wilderness is recognized as describing places where human dominion is not absolute, even though these are lands we might visit often and form intense connections with. What's our motivation for going there, and what do we expect to find when we do?

Knowledge of environmental ethics gives us perspective on how value, or philosophical worth, is assessed between humans and nature. For wilderness, we examine values, or standards, and support these through an ethic. A high-quality wilderness experience is dependent on attributes such as intact natural settings and conditions, solitude, physical challenge, and unique and fulfilling experience. A well-developed wildland ethic would protect the factors that enable these.

The Wilderness Act outlines a set of conditions for wilderness: untrammeled (unrestrained), primeval character and influence, without permanent improvements or

Wildlands ethics proceed from the assumption that the wilderness is intrinsically good and valuable.

human habitation, and preserved natural conditions. It also provides for qualities of wilderness, such as "outstanding opportunities for solitude, or a primitive and unconfined type of recreation."[61] These are familiar characteristics, and they hold great importance. Nonetheless, despite the ambitious intent of the act, defining wilderness is an extremely difficult thing to do. Its appeal is universal, but what specifically makes it what it is, and how do we catalog all of its values?

For framing the fundamental values of wilderness, a comparison of use versus nonuse attributes is sometimes useful.[62] Use is categorized by activities such as recreation, outfitting, grazing, and consumptive resource extraction. Nonuse values are readily recognizable: scenic beauty, preserved ecosystems, spiritual inspiration, wildlife and endangered species habitat, preservation for future generations, and the vicarious benefit of simply knowing that the wildland is there.

Wilderness managers take stock of the state of the wildland resource and look at the threats that encumber its values. Tangible and visible concerns—air quality, ecological damage, livestock grazing, wildland fire, and invasive species—engender action. Less distinct values, such as solitude and primitive experience, remoteness, and a climate of spiritual enrichment, are more difficult to assess and manage effectively.

The economic standpoint of a wilderness is also considered. Studies have provided valuable insight by quantifying the dollar value of recreation, tourism, science, and "ecological services," which include watersheds, air quality, nutrient cycling, carbon storage, and wildlife habitat.[63] Efforts at placing monetary value on wilderness are not very operative in developing an ethic, but they are much needed in reacting to societal and political systems that stumble over qualitative, nonuse attributes. A view toward the panoply of threats to wilderness makes identifying this dollar value a powerful tactic in its protection.

For some, a mere listing of wilderness attributes is a bit less useful in explaining the "stuff" of wilderness. The Wilderness Act declares that we must preserve wilderness character. On one hand, this incorporates stewardship of the land. But wilderness character also necessitates an understanding of the human experience in wilderness and the relationships people form with it. Environmental author and educator Michael Frome explains that wilderness is a place of more abstract, all-encompassing values:

> Wilderness areas are not playgrounds, nor theme parks, but sanctuaries, meant to be forever; they are priceless time capsules for tomorrow that we are privileged to know and enjoy today. By that I mean a wilderness is ideally suited to exercise the body in a test with nature, stimulate the mind with new learning, and challenge the spirit of the individual to connect with something larger than himself or herself, and more lasting than all the mechanization of life and work at home.[64]

Frome's evaluation is supported by the relatively recent proliferation of wildland-based experiential and therapeutic programs, along with a growing understanding of the spiritual benefits of wilderness.

Laura and Guy Waterman pioneered the examination of wilderness and wildland ethics in the mountains of New England, and their work looks at the intangibles we risk losing when faced with overcrowded, heavily

Leave No Trace has worked succesfully to bring wilderness values and low-impact practices to the public.

impacted, and overmanaged wilderness. Laura Waterman defines these values—qualities such as freedom and the sense of adventure and discovery—as the "spirit of wildness" and warns that they are at great risk today.[65]

In the early 1990s, the Forest Service instituted its Leave No Trace (LNT) initiative. Through regionally molded sets of guidelines, LNT aims to educate wilderness visitors about low-impact behaviors or skills and highly ethical use of wildlands. As a partner in this venture, the National Outdoor Leadership School (NOLS) develops LNT curriculum and offers training in skills and ethics for a wide variety of wilderness regions. In the years following, the Bureau of Land Management, National Park Service, U.S. Fish and Wildlife Service, and myriad other business, educational, and organizational partners joined the effort, and LNT has grown into a strong and vitally important component in the stewardship of wildlands and development of outdoor ethics. Driven by impacts resulting from nonmechanized use of wildlands, the current mission of the Leave No Trace Center for Outdoor Ethics, the organization that oversees the program, is "promoting and inspiring responsible outdoor recreation through education, research and partnerships."[66] Today it is standard practice among managing agencies, permittees, outdoor programs, and wilderness visitors to practice and promote LNT skills. It is an important element in outlining and protecting values and the human experience in wilderness. LNT has seven principles:

- Plan ahead and prepare.
- Travel and camp on durable surfaces.
- Dispose of waste properly.
- Leave what you find.
- Minimize campfire impacts.
- Respect wildlife.
- Be considerate of other visitors.

A large part of the utility of LNT is that it embraces behaviors that honor the full spectrum of wilderness values. It encourages the application of skills that protect the environment, wildlife, esthetics, cultural resources, and social values. It also recognizes the value of research in determining the best approaches to reducing or eliminating our impacts on wildlands. With strong educational and research components, LNT is helping to affect people's behaviors in wilderness and to form responsible wildland ethics.

An understanding of wilderness values is a first step in building a personal wildland ethic. But wilderness means different things to different people. Purposeful reflection helps one examine and internalize one's own valuation of wilderness. One exercise, developed by the Forest Service, asks several questions such as the following:

- Do you feel it is OK to maintain historic cabins in wilderness?
- Do you feel it is appropriate to control predators in wilderness that are killing a substantial number of livestock?
- Do you feel it is OK to have trail signs in wilderness?
- Do you feel we should be protecting known threatened and endangered species habitat from prescribed natural fires?[67]

Designed as a tool to help managers understand and identify their personal orientation and underlying philosophy toward wilderness, this exercise has universal application and invites the public to consider evolving issues such as fixed rock-climbing anchors, permit systems, and cell-phone use. As people examine their personal ethics, it often becomes apparent that hard choices must be made in taking right actions, and that decisions between right and wrong are often not black and white, but gray.

As we evolve and grow, in age, education, experience, and perspective, we should expect change in what we value in wilderness and seek change in our ethics. The good company of kindred souls along the Appalachian Trail may have led us to acceptance of seeing other people in wilderness. Better camp stoves and an understanding of wildland impacts might have made us less reliant on campfires.

One of the most vivid portrayals of major change in personal values and ethics is presented by Aldo Leopold in "Thinking like a Mountain." In this essay, which reflects on humility and learning from mistakes, Leopold returns to an evolution of his understanding of nature from his early days as a game warden, when good wildlife management encouraged the killing of predators. He describes a dying mother wolf whom he had shot and the realization that her death brought to him: that the howl of the wolf was really a symbol of healthy wildland.

My own conviction on this score dates from the day I saw a wolf die. We were eating lunch on a high rimrock, at the foot of which a turbulent river elbowed its way. We saw what we thought was a doe fording the torrent, her breast awash in white water. When she climbed the bank toward us and shook out her tail, we realized our error: it was a wolf. A half-dozen others, evidently grown pups, sprang from the willows and all joined in a welcoming melee of wagging tails and playful maulings. What was literally a pile of wolves writhed and tumbled in the center of an open flat at the foot of our rimrock.

In those days we had never heard of passing up a chance to kill a wolf. In a second we were pumping lead into the pack, but with more excitement than accuracy: how to aim a steep downhill shot is always confusing. When our rifles were empty, the old wolf was down, and a pup was dragging a leg into impassable slide-rocks.

We reached the old wolf in time to watch a fierce green fire dying in her eyes. I realized then, and have known ever since, that there was something new to me in those eyes—something known only to her and to the mountain. I was young then, and full of trigger-itch; I thought that because fewer wolves meant more deer, that no wolves would mean hunters' paradise. But after seeing the green fire die, I sensed that neither the wolf nor the mountain agreed with such a view.[68]

Wilderness ethics are an important part of the curriculum at NOLS.

5

The Role of Wilderness Education

Those of us with a stake in the future of wilderness must begin to develop . . . an agenda which will place a clear, strong, national focus on the question of the responsibility of the wilderness user to wilderness.

—Paul Petzoldt

EDUCATING FOR ETHICS

Can we teach ethics? To achieve consensus and disseminate knowledge effectively in our society requires the participation of all its systems and institutions—educational, political, religious, and economic. One look around would seem to indicate that educating people about their connection and consequent responsibilities to the earth is a monumental undertaking. On the other hand, such an education is probably the only viable means through which long-term changes in societal values can be effected.

What is the necessary business of education in the evolution of a wildland ethic? Regarding the evolution of ethics in general, Charles Darwin writes, "As soon as a virtue is honoured and practiced by some few men, it spreads through instruction and example to the young, and eventually becomes incorporated in public opinion."[69] Ethics evolve, therefore, much as physical characteristics do.

Though education is often a slow and perhaps inefficient means to an end, it is nonetheless a critical one. Ethics evolve, but the guidance, reinforcement, and encouragement of society play a critical role in this evolution. Programs that have found success in outdoor ethics education focus on supportive social environments that promote individual character development. Environmental educators Harold Hungerford and Trudi Volk point out critical educational components that research shows can maximize behavioral changes from environmental education:

- Teach significant ethical concepts, and make clear the learner's relationship and obligation to them.
- Provide carefully designed and in-depth opportunities for learners to develop an ethical sensitivity to the environment, to the outdoor activity they're involved with, and to each other. This promotes a desire to behave appropriately.
- Provide a curriculum that teaches learners the critical thinking skills they need to analyze issues and investigate ethical problems. Provide the time to apply these skills.
- Provide a curriculum that will teach learners the citizenship (stewardship) and interpersonal skills they need to address and resolve ethical issues. Provide the time to apply these skills.
- Provide a learning setting which offers the learner consistent reinforcement for acting responsibly (thus allowing him to develop his own sense of ethics).[70]

In wilderness education, the whole of the outdoors effectively becomes the classroom.

Public land managers have a mandate to maintain wildlands at a certain level of ecological health and, often, visual and esthetic purity. They have many tools from which to choose to encourage backcountry visitors to protect the land, including rules, regulations, and educational efforts. Backcountry travelers are often seeking adventure, independence, and solitude and might therefore resent an abundance of rules that dictate where, when, and how they may travel. Educating wildland visitors is often a viable and preferable alternative to restrictive regulations for preserving wild places.

People can learn to value, respect, and take care of wildlands. Intellectual discourse is interesting and can give shape to new ideas, and individuals can cogitate at length about ethics and wildness, but the best place to learn about one's own wildland ethic is on the land. There is no real substitute for time spent in the backcountry.

LESSONS IN NATURE

Nature has infinite lessons to teach human beings seeking to nurture or redefine their relationship with it. Wildlands are classrooms in which we are students of nature and of ourselves. Natural processes in a myriad of ecosystems demonstrate the interconnectedness of species, including humans. Outdoor education is uniquely spontaneous, and instructors can make the best use of their classroom by being responsive to this, taking advantage of teachable moments, which the backcountry offers aplenty.

Nature has many ecological lessons to teach humans, but it also addresses us on other levels. Time spent in the backcountry helps maintain and rejuvenate our sense of wonder. "The faculty of wonder tires easily," writes Joseph Wood Krutch in *The Desert Year*, "and a miracle which happens everyday is a miracle no longer, no matter how many times one tells oneself that it ought to be."[71] Just when you think you have become too jaded to marvel over another spectacular sunset, nature surprises you with one not quite like any other you've seen. And once again you marvel and become mindful of your connection with the earth.

In sharing your wonder about a place with others, it is reaffirmed and maintained within yourself. This process is self-perpetuating: You see the wilderness anew when you look at it through the fresh eyes of a student, a fledgling wilderness traveler. By stimulating the faculties of curiosity and wonder in students, the instructor may contribute to a lifelong pattern for both teacher and student.

WILDERNESS EDUCATION

Wilderness educators are in a unique position to contribute to the evolution of a wildland ethic, and the

NOLS founder Paul Petzoldt saw education as a vital part of preserving the wilderness for future generations.

SKIP SHOUTIS

potential contributions include several distinct components. It is the duty of these instructors to teach students that the privilege of wilderness travel carries with it responsibilities.

First, wilderness educators can teach people to live and travel in the backcountry in a manner that will leave the least impact. Minimum-impact camping techniques are essential to wilderness preservation. These skills make it possible for people to travel through wildlands in a manner that leaves virtually no visual or ecological impact. As a result, all backcountry visitors have the opportunity to experience a similar sense of discovery and are encouraged to implement Leave No Trace practices, a skill set that fosters ecological health.

The second component is when students find ways to transfer skills and values acquired in the backcountry to

their lives elsewhere. A wilderness educational experience is an opportunity for students to live simply in and
with wilderness, which can cultivate a new kind of
awareness. If you can live comfortably out of a backpack
for four weeks, then surely you don't *need* all the trappings with which we surround ourselves most of the
time. The immediacy of the feedback the wilderness environment provides helps people establish habits of self-
scrutiny and careful decision making. Students might
then decide to apply those habits to their daily lives and
begin to think in terms of walking softly everywhere they
go. NOLS instructor Morgan Hite reflected on these ideas
of transference while working a course in Wyoming's
Wind River Mountains:

> People always talk about what you can't take
> home after a NOLS course. You can't take home
> the backpack, or at least it has no place in your
> daily life. You can't take home the rations, and if
> you did, your friends wouldn't eat them. You
> can't take home the mountains. All our connec-
> tions to this place and our experiences here we
> seem to have to get rid of. It's frustrating and it
> can be depressing.
>
> This essay is about what you can take home.
> What you can take home, and what, if you work
> at it, can be more important than any of those
> things you have to leave behind.
>
> Let's look at what we've really been doing out
> here. We've been organized: we lived out of back-
> packs the whole time, and mostly we knew where
> everything was. We've been thorough: we
> counted every little contour line on the map and
> put every little bit of trash in a bag. We've been

prepared: at this very moment every one of us knows where his or her raingear is. We've taken chances with other people, entrusted them with our lives and seen no reason not to grow close to them. We've persevered and put our minds to things that never seemed to end. We've learned to use new tools and new techniques. We've taken care of the things we have with us. We've lived simply. . . .

Remember you can let go and do without seemingly crucial things. Here it has only been hot showers, forks and a roof overhead. . . . It is good to remember that letting go and doing without has never ruled out joy.[72]

Instructors can also help students find ways to actually enhance the overall health and sustainability of the wilderness through which they travel. This might mean a day spent cleaning and rehabilitating a heavily used campsite, exploring ways they can share the lessons of minimum-impact camping with friends at home, or providing them with the tools and knowledge necessary to become effective, informed participants in the management of public lands.

Wilderness educators also should be able to give students a glimpse of their own commitment to and passion for wild places. There is a place for passion. Cool analysis may be an important component of the defense of wildlands where the battles are the most crucial, but that analysis must be fueled by passionate conviction, or it becomes meaningless and ineffective. Darwin told us that virtue is spread through instruction and example before it becomes incorporated into public opinion. Thus it is the responsibility of educators to teach through both. Passion for wilderness, constructively channeled and effectively communicated, will constitute a cogent example for students approaching a new set of ideas.

PERSONAL RESPONSIBILITY

An instructive activity that is helpful to many outdoor programs is the campsite check, wherein a group of students and one or two instructors walk around to each campsite after folks have packed up. The purpose of the check is to survey the area—to see how the campers have done in their efforts to minimize impact. The activity has no formal agenda; the group looks for overturned rocks, matted grass or wildflowers, bits of garbage or food, or any other sign that someone has camped there, and then talks about whether these impacts are ecological or merely esthetic.

It is not often that people get such immediate feedback about their impacts or, conversely, their ability to walk softly. The campsite check provides a convenient starting point for broader discussions about minimum-impact living. What are the practical implications of a wildland ethic to the individual? First, it seems, is to recognize one's impacts on the land, both direct while in the backcountry and indirect as a result of daily habits in one's home life. The next step is to decide if they are acceptable. If they are not, the third step is to reduce those impacts.

Direct impacts on wildlands and other visitors are usually easy to recognize, although they may also be quite subtle. Minimizing one's impact in the backcountry is largely a matter of technique and awareness, but an ethic usually provides the motivation for specific Leave No Trace skills, since they generally require a bit more care and effort than other camping practices.

On a larger scale, a wildland ethic must be part of a more encompassing land or environmental ethic that is expressed every day. You can continue to minimize your impacts on the land after you leave the backcountry and return to civilization. Aldo Leopold provides a basic guideline for examining your consumptive habits and daily life in his counsel on the rightness of preserving the biotic community. We have considerable freedom in this country to make lifestyle choices that reflect our personal ethics.

The 1973 book by the British economist E. F. Schumacher, *Small Is Beautiful,* addresses this notion of lifestyle from a more global, cross-cultural perspective. Schumacher, like the deep ecologists, encourages us to critically examine the basic assumptions underlying our society:

The cultivation and expansion of needs is the antithesis of wisdom. It is also the antithesis of freedom and peace. Every increase of needs tends to increase one's dependence on outside forces over which one cannot have control, and therefore increases existential fear. Only by a reduction of needs can one promote a genuine reduction in those tensions, which are the ultimate causes of strife and war. . . . How could we even begin to disarm greed and envy? Perhaps by being much less greedy and envious ourselves; perhaps by resisting the temptation of letting our luxuries become needs; and perhaps by even scrutinizing our needs to see if they cannot be simplified and reduced. . . . An ounce of practice is generally worth more than a ton of theory.[73]

But what does that "ounce of practice" entail? How can you simplify and reduce and thereby begin to walk more softly? Author and farmer Wendell Berry writes of the practical implications of a land ethic: "To use or not to use nature is not a choice that is available to us; we can live only at the expense of other lives. Our choice has rather to do with how and how much to use. And this is not a choice that can be satisfactorily decided in principle or in theory. This is not a choice that can be satisfactorily decided in principle or in theory; it is a choice intransigently practical. It must be worked out in local practice."[74]

The lifestyle choices and changes suggested by Schumacher and Berry are not new or radical. Others before them from different times and cultures, such as Henry David Thoreau, Mohandas Gandhi, and Jesus Christ, have espoused simple living and self-restraint. What is new is the underlying ecological conscience. In response to the statement that humans must exploit wilderness for resources to maintain our standard of living, the venerable environmentalist David Brower says that a viable, if often overlooked, alternative is to lower that standard.

PUTTING ETHICS INTO PRACTICE

Though certain modes and patterns of behavior are held to be acceptable in wilderness, a target wildland ethic cannot realistically be defined for any individual. Just as the path each hiker opts to take through the mountains is an individual choice, every person's ethic is a unique set of values, choices, and judgmental decisions. It is possible, however, to establish general goals for wildland ethics that speak to the desired condition and virtues of wilderness, ecology, and the natural world. It is these goals that are all-important. A strong wildland ethic asks that in wilderness, you do the following:

LORI A. DAVIS

- Look beyond yourself and consider the existence, virtues, and value of other creatures, organisms, ecological processes, and all the features of the landscape.
- Consider your goals and reasons for visiting these lands and weigh these against the impacts of your actions.
- Respect the human connection to wilderness—the spirituality and refreshment that it offers and the opportunity to reconnect with elements of the human condition that are unavailable in our modern and familiar world.
- Think not only of the present condition of wildlands, but also of the past and, most important, the future.
- Accept that in seeking wilderness, you seek requisite challenge.

- Respect and protect the rights of others to experience wilderness uninfluenced by your actions.
- Seek to learn, observe, and actively question your values, achieving personal growth as your relationship with wildlands develops.
- Actively examine your values relative to the condition of wilderness and examine the influence of change on these values.
- Seek to revel in the human spirit of adventure, but always respect that your adventures are often made possible by the provisions of wilderness, and that what you are given should not go unrequited.
- Strive to establish an ethic based on caring, humility, and the honest application of judgment.
- Remember that your own ethic, however manifest, will always be reflected in your conduct.

While the wheels of change in our society sometimes turn slowly and inefficiently, they do produce results, and ethics can become global norms. Things we now take for granted, such as recycling, Earth Day, unleaded gasoline, and the Environmental Protection Agency did not exist fifty years ago. Leave No Trace is no longer just a good idea; it is a creed. Change happens. Whatever the pace, the development and advancement of ethics *do* work to help resolve the problems the environment faces.

It's important to remember where you've come from and who and what has influenced your life. The everyday choices you make are, in essence, the exercise of your personal legacy. This legacy may include great people, beautiful places, and life-shaping events. These things have become part of you, just as the wildlands you visit become part of your soul. If you believe in the importance of wildlands and their irrefutable effect on the human condition, then you must also offer them the best of your human capabilities—understanding, caring, and stewardship. To put wildland ethics into practice, each of us must do our part in ensuring that wild nature will remain.

Keep the lessons simple, but carry them with you on your travels and teach them to others—for the good of the wild places that make us, and this earth, complete.

PART TWO

Wilderness Management in the United States

Together, the land management agencies of the federal government oversee nearly 700 million acres of public land.

6

Federal Land Management

The Congress shall have Power to dispose of and make all needful Rules and Regulations respecting the Territory or other Property belonging to the United States.

—U.S. Constitution

From this deceptively simple line in the Constitution of the United States, stewardship of our nation's wildlands has evolved into a complex undertaking. An impressive array of factors has shaped this evolution, ranging from legislative mandate and legal decisions to social values, economic objectives, attitudes, politics, and lifestyles. Over the years, land management guiding principles and policies have varied and shifted in response to all of these variables. The idea during the settlement of this country that wilderness was dangerous and forbidding has slowly transformed into the belief that it is essential and that some lands must be preserved in their natural condition. But there remains a wide range of opinion about what it means to manage public land for the greater good.

In the mid-1900s, land management began to shift from active disposal of public lands into private hands—

Principal Land Management Responsibilities within the Federal Government

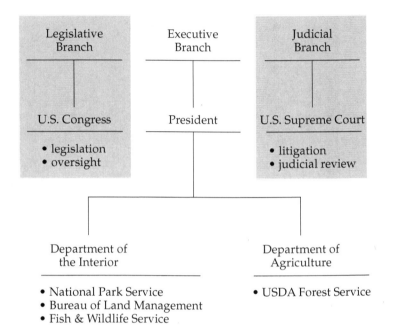

Legislative Branch	Executive Branch	Judicial Branch
U.S. Congress	President	U.S. Supreme Court
• legislation • oversight		• litigation • judicial review

Department of the Interior	Department of Agriculture
• National Park Service • Bureau of Land Management • Fish & Wildlife Service	• USDA Forest Service

a mechanism to encourage settlement in the nineteenth century—to active management of wild areas held in the public trust. While laws, regulations, and policies provide the legal structure for land management, human ethics, values, and emotions play a vital role in how we regard, protect, and manage our limited resource of public land.

This section of the book places public lands and wilderness in the current legal and policy context by outlining the unique mission, responsibilities, management styles, and challenges of each of the four major government agencies charged with caring for federal land. The brief survey presented here can only begin to explore wildlands history and policy. We hope that you will continue to learn and exercise the rights and responsibilities of citizens to effect positive changes in the ways our nation manages its natural resources.

WHAT ARE THE NATION'S PUBLIC LANDS?

A number of agencies manage federal land with missions as different as the Everglades of Florida are from the deserts of Utah. These agencies are stewards for hundreds of millions of acres, employ tens of thousands of people, and work with budgets totaling billions of dollars. Federal land provides the country with numerous benefits: renewable and nonrenewable commodities, extensive recreation opportunities, wildlife and wildlife habitat, educational and scientific resources, airshed and watershed protection, to name a few. The agencies are challenged with managing the land in accordance with their missions to ensure that these benefits endure.

The federal government owns roughly 672 million acres of public land, or 30 percent of the 2.3 billion acres of land in the United States.[75] Of this, 628 million acres (93 percent) falls within the scope of just four agencies: the USDA Forest Service, in the Department of Agriculture; and the National Park Service (NPS), Bureau of Land Management (BLM), and Fish and Wildlife Service (FWS), in the Department of the Interior. The remaining land is spread among several agencies, including the Bureau of Reclamation, Bureau of Indian Affairs, Department of Defense, and Tennessee Valley Authority.

This vast acreage has grown over time. In the 1800s, seven of the original thirteen colonies ceded their western lands to the federal government as part of a compromise with the smaller colonies to garner support for signing the Articles of Confederation. These lands, lying between

Agency Jurisdiction over Federal Lands

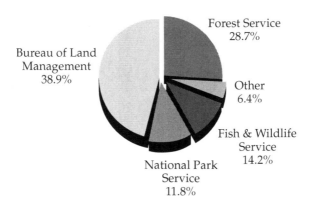

Forest Service
28.7%

Bureau of Land
Management
38.9%

Other
6.4%

Fish & Wildlife
Service
14.2%

National Park
Service
11.8%

Percentage of Each Agency's Land
that is Designated Wilderness

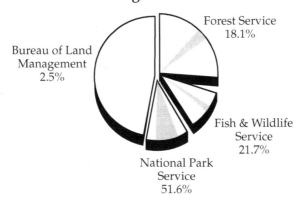

Forest Service
18.1%

Bureau of Land
Management
2.5%

Fish & Wildlife
Service
21.7%

National Park
Service
51.6%

the Appalachian Mountains and the Mississippi River, formed the vast majority of federal holdings in the young nation.

Lands between the Mississippi River and the Pacific coast were acquired through a series of purchases and treaties, such as the Louisiana Purchase of 1803 and

Percentage of Federal Land in Each State

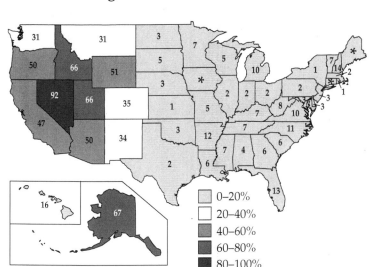

treaties with Mexico and Great Britain. The annexation of Texas completed the territory that would become the Lower 48 states in 1845. The purchase of Alaska from Russia in 1867 added the largest parcel to the federal real estate inventory—more than 365 million acres.

In 1812, the Department of the Interior created the General Land Office to oversee the disposal of hundreds of millions of acres by transferring ownership to private or state hands under the authority of the Homestead Act. For nearly two centuries, this transfer effort was the predominant federal land policy. From the late 1700s through 2002, 816 million acres were transferred to private ownership. Another 455 million acres were taken over by states. Most of this activity occurred before 1940.[76] The land that is now the public domain consists of what remained of the original acquisitions at the conclusion of the era of disposal.

Federally Owned Land by State, as of September 30, 2003

State	Total Acreage	Acreage of Federally Owned Land	Percentage of State that is Federal Land
Alabama	32,678,400	1,202,614	3.7
Alaska	365,481,600	243,847,037	66.7
Arizona	72,688,000	36,494,844	50.2
Arkansas	33,599,360	3,955,959	11.8
California	100,206,720	46,979,891	46.9
Colorado	66,485,760	23,174,340	34.9
Connecticut	3,135,360	15,212	0.5
Delaware	1,265,920	29,488	2.3
District of Columbia	39,040	10,284	26.3
Florida	34,721,280	4,605,762	13.3
Georgia	37,295,360	2,314,386	6.2
Hawaii	4,105,600	671,580	16.4
Idaho	52,933,120	35,135,709	66.4
Illinois	35,795,200	651,603	1.8
Indiana	23,158,400	534,126	2.3
Iowa	35,860,480	302,601	0.8
Kansas	52,510,720	641,562	1.2
Kentucky	25,512,320	1,706,562	6.7
Louisiana	28,867,840	1,501,735	5.2
Maine	19,847,680	164,003	0.8
Maryland	6,319,360	192,692	3.0
Massachusetts	5,034,880	105,973	2.1
Michigan	36,492,160	3,638,588	10.0
Minnesota	51,205,760	3,534,989	6.9
Mississippi	30,222,720	2,101,204	7.0
Missouri	44,248,320	2,237,951	5.1
Montana	93,271,040	29,239,058	31.3
Nebraska	49,031,680	1,458,802	3.0
Nevada	70,264,320	64,689,139	91.9
New Hampshire	5,768,960	830,232	14.4
New Jersey	4,813,440	180,189	3.7
New Mexico	77,766,400	26,518,360	34.1
New York	30,680,960	242,441	0.8
North Carolina	31,402,880	3,602,080	11.5
North Dakota	44,452,480	1,333,375	3.0
Ohio	26,222,080	457,697	1.7
Oklahoma	44,087,680	1,331,457	3.0
Oregon	61,598,720	30,638,949	49.7
Pennsylvania	28,804,480	724,925	2.5
Rhode Island	677,120	5,318	0.8
South Carolina	19,374,080	1,236,214	6.4
South Dakota	48,881,920	2,314,007	4.7
Tennessee	26,727,680	2,016,138	7.5
Texas	168,217,600	3,171,757	1.9
Utah	52,696,9600	35,024,927	66.5
Vermont	5,936,640	450,017	7.6
Virginia	25,496,320	2,617,226	10.3
Washington	42,693,760	13,246,559	31.0
West Virginia	15,410,560	1,266,422	8.2
Wisconsin	35,011,200	1,981,781	5.7
Wyoming	62,343,040	31,531,537	50.6
TOTAL	**2,271,343,360**	**671,759,298**	**29.6**

Source: Vincent et al., *CRS Report for Congress*.

In the twentieth century, emphasis shifted from disposal to the retention and management of public land. The underlying philosophy of eminent domain had been satisfied—settlement had reached the West Coast. A need for timber and a growing rift between the federal government and private landowners, most commonly over rangeland use, helped solidify this shift. Congress passed laws, such as the Payment in Lieu of Taxes Act (PILT), to require the federal government to share revenue with states and local governments in which the federal land was located. Barring a significant change in administrative policy, most of the 672 million acres that now remain in federal hands will be actively managed by the federal agencies well into the future. This shift in policy is reflected clearly in the following clause in the Federal Land Policy and Management Act of 1976 (FLPMA): "The Congress declares that it is the policy of the United States that (1) the public lands be retained in Federal ownership, unless as a result of the land use planning procedure provided for in this Act, it is determined that disposal of a particular parcel will serve the national interest."[77]

Dynamic cultural change in America has created conditions in which the four agencies now fill unique management niches. As time goes on, the forces of political will and social pressure will continue to shape the evolution of land management.

MAJOR STATUTES GOVERNING LAND MANAGEMENT

1862 Homestead Act: Signed by President Abraham Lincoln; turned over vast amounts of the public domain to private hands. In total, 270 million acres were claimed under the act.

1872 Mining Act: Established a process to allow private prospecting and development of mineral resources on all public lands. The act states "that all valuable mineral deposits in lands belonging to the United States, both surveyed and unsurveyed, are hereby declared to be free and open to exploration and purchase."

1872 Yellowstone National Park Act: Provides much of the language used in legislation to establish subsequent national parks. Yellowstone was established to serve as a "public park or pleasuring ground for the benefit and enjoyment of the people."

1891 Forest Reserve Act: Established authority to set aside forest reserves. An amendment to the bill authorized the president to "set apart and reserve . . . any part of the public lands wholly or in part covered with timber or undergrowth, whether of commercial value or not, as public reservations."

1897 Organic Administration Act: Provided the first forest reserve management guidelines, defining the priority uses of the reserves to be watershed protection and timber production.

1905 Reorganization Act: Transferred the management of the forest reserves to the Department of Agriculture, thus creating the Forest Service.

1911 Weeks Act: Directed the Secretary of Agriculture to permanently purchase, reserve, hold, and administer private lands as National Forests.

1916 National Park Service Organic Act: Established the National Park Service within the Department of the Interior. The purpose of the units—national parks, monuments, and other designated lands—is "to conserve the scenery and the natural and historic objects and the wild life therein and to provide for the enjoyment of the same in such manner and by such means as will leave them unimpaired for future generations."

1934 Taylor Grazing Act: Ended the wholesale disposal of federal lands into private or state ownership, creating the Grazing Service to manage 142 million acres of federal lands that had been parceled into grazing districts. The roots of the modern Bureau of Land Management are found in this act.

1956 Fish and Wildlife Act: Reorganized federal wildlife management and created the U.S. Fish and Wildlife Service.

1960 Multiple-Use Sustained Yield Act: Established multiple use and a sustained yield of renewable resources as the policy of the Forest Service. The act states, "It is the policy of the Congress that the national forests are established and shall be administered for outdoor recreation, range, timber, watershed, and wildlife and fish purposes."

1963 Outdoor Recreation Act: Established the Interior Department's role as coordinator of all federal agencies for programs affecting the conservation and development of recreation resources, directing the secretary of the interior to prepare a nationwide recreation plan that promotes the conservation and use of recreation resources.

1964 Wilderness Act: Created the National Wilderness Preservation System. Today the system is composed of portions of national forest, national park, national wildlife refuge, and BLM lands known as Wilderness areas.

1966 National Wildlife Refuge System Administration Act: Established the National Wildlife Refuge System under the management of the FWS.

1969 National Environmental Policy Act (NEPA): Established a land management planning process that mandates public participation and environmental analyses such as environmental impact statements (EISs) and environmental assessments (EAs). NEPA's purpose is "to declare a national policy which will encourage productive and enjoyable harmony between man and his environment; [and] to promote efforts which will prevent or eliminate damage to the environment and biosphere and stimulate the health and welfare of man."

1973 Endangered Species Act: Established standards by which agencies, landowners, and citizens will protect and restore endangered species and their habitat based on three elements: listing a species as threatened or endangered; designating habitat essential for survival and recovery; and restoring healthy populations so a species can be removed from designation.

1974 Forest Rangeland Renewable Resources Planning Act: Specified that land and resource management plans are to be developed for forest and rangeland renewable resources. This and the National Forest Management Act of 1976 serve as the foundation for Forest Service planning activities.

1975 Eastern Wilderness Areas Act: Extended wilderness designation to the first Forest Service lands in the East and clarified congressional direction to the managing agencies.

1976 Federal Land Policy and Management Act: Established guidelines for the administration and conservation of public lands managed by the BLM.

1976 Payments in Lieu of Taxes Act: Established that payments be made to local governments to compensate for the tax-exempt status of federal land. Payments are made in addition to any revenue sharing associated with the sale of resources developed from the land.

1976 National Forest Management Act: Created a detailed set of management plans for the Forest Service and mandated the consideration of all multiple-use values in regional guides and forest plans.

1980 Alaska National Interest Lands Conservation Act (ANILCA): Classified vast portions of public lands in Alaska as national parks, national preserves, national forests, national wildlife refuges, and Wilderness areas. ANILCA set up guidelines for future use, including conservation and disposal to state ownership of federal lands in Alaska.

7

National
Forests

Established:	1905 by the Reorganization Act
Administering agency:	U.S. Department of Agriculture
Responsibility:	National forests and grasslands
Total acreage:	192.5 million acres[78]
Wilderness:	34.9 million acres
Budget (FY 2004):	$4.54 billion[79]
Employees (FY 2005):	32,000 permanent[80]
Website:	www.fs.fed.us
Mission:	To sustain the health, diversity, and productivity of the nation's forests and grasslands to meet the needs of present and future generations; caring for the land and serving people

National forests today are valued for the wide variety of benefits they provide. Timber production, energy and minerals development, and grazing offer commodities demanded by our continually growing economy. Forests shelter wildlife, preserve watersheds, and hold stands of trees that help cleanse the air we breathe, and they also

USDA FOREST SERVICE

provide the setting for a wide range of recreational activities, such as hunting and fishing, camping, backpacking, rock climbing, mountain bicycling, skiing, horse packing, wildlife viewing, and motorized sports. Wilderness areas within national forests preserve wildlands in their natural condition.

Allowing for all of these interests on national forest land is known as multiple use, a term often employed to describe the overall mission of the Forest Service, as mandated by Congress. This was not always the agency's mission; it took years for the philosophy to evolve, and the Forest Service continues to struggle with accommodating the range of uses for national forests required by law.

HISTORY OF THE FOREST SERVICE

The agency's roots can be traced to the 1880s and 1890s, when its mission was focused on two resources: watersheds and timber. Two schools of thought emerged regarding how best to manage the forests. One, led by Gifford Pinchot, supported managing forests for sustainable grazing, timber harvest, and mining. The second, led by John Muir, emphasized watershed protection and preservation. This debate, though shaped by new issues and regulations, continues today.

By the last decade of the nineteenth century, concern over the rapid pace of deforestation led Congress to authorize the president to establish forest reserves. The Organic Administration Act of 1897 provided the first forest reserve management guidelines: reserves were to be managed to provide for high-quality watersheds and a continuous supply of timber. But the act also stated that management must "preserve the living and growing timber," thus beginning Congress's effort to balance the need for timber with the need to preserve forests.

In 1905, Congress passed the Reorganization Act, which transferred responsibility for the reserves to the Department of Agriculture and created the Forest Service. Gifford Pinchot was installed as its first chief. As a student of European scientific forestry, Pinchot embodied a philosophical commitment to the role of conservation and adopted utilitarian use of forests as his guiding principle. A letter ghostwritten by Pinchot for Secretary of Agriculture James Wilson on the day the Reorganization Act was passed outlines Pinchot's management approach and the mission of the Forest Service. It has served as the touchstone for modern multiple-use management. It reads in part:

In the administration of the forest reserves it must be clearly borne in mind that all land is to be devoted to its most productive use for the permanent good of the whole people, and not for the temporary benefit of individuals or companies. All the resources of the reserves are for use, and this use must be brought about in a thoroughly prompt and businesslike manner, under such restrictions only as will insure the permanence of these resources . . . always bearing in mind that the conservative use of these resources in no way conflicts with their permanent value.

In the management of each reserve, local questions will be decided upon local grounds; the dominant industry will be considered first, but with as little restriction to minor industries as may be possible . . . and where conflicting interests must be reconciled, the question will always be decided from the standpoint of the greatest good of the greatest number in the long run.

This strong utilitarian mandate, expressed in Pinchot's now-famous phrasing of providing "the greatest good of the greatest number in the long run," molded the Forest Service's view of its mission. Forests were to be managed for the enrichment of society. But this notion threatened westerners, who believed that the federal government had no right to such heavy-handed management.

The domain of national forests marched eastward with the passage of the Weeks Act in 1911. A series of devastating eastern floods caused lawmakers to see the need to protect watersheds from overcutting. The act authorized federal funds to purchase degraded lands to be reforested by the Forest Service. Over the next thirty years, twenty-six new forests were established in the East. By the mid-twentieth century, the purpose of national forests had broadened from watershed and timber production to include grazing, wildlife, and recreation. Demand for new homes in the United States and lumber to rebuild Europe in the wake of World War II sent the annual timber harvest soaring from 3.5 billion board feet in 1950 to more than 8 billion in 1959. At the same time, postwar Americans took to outdoor recreation more than any previous generation. The Forest Service found itself squeezed by competing interests. Timber, grazing, recreation, minerals, and wilderness interests impaired the agency's ability to satisfy all users.

Relief came in the form of the Multiple-Use Sustained Yield Act of 1960 (MUSYA), which established the range of fundamental multiple-use values. The act states that "national forests are established and shall be administered for outdoor recreation, range, timber, watershed, and wildlife and fish purposes."[81] For the first time, the Forest Service had the power of statutory mandate to support it when facing interests demanding single-use management. Subsequent acts of Congress further defined the agency's responsibilities. These include the Wilderness Act of 1964, which added wilderness to the range of uses for which forests must be managed, as well as the National Environmental Policy Act, Endangered Species Act, Clean Air Act, and Clean Water Act.

Many current issues and challenges facing the Forest Service result from the dichotomy between its utilitarian roots and the expansion of its mission to include nonutilitarian values. A mandate to protect the natural character of wilderness, for example, complicates management that traditionally emphasized the production of goods. The addition of numerous layers of statutory responsibility, while helping guide agency management, has also led to a feeling within the agency and among its critics that the Forest Service has been bogged down in administrative obligation. As the twenty-first century begins, the agency is embarking on an effort to streamline the processes that it believes have led to legal gridlock and impeded good and timely management of its lands.

ORGANIZATION
The Forest Service administers three principal programs: the National Forest System, State and Private Forestry, and Forestry Research. In addition, international forest programs play a more prominent role as the nation moves rapidly into a global commodities marketplace. The agency sells timber, manages recreation sites, builds and maintains roads and trails, manages livestock grazing and fish and wildlife habitat, fights fires, and controls invasive species. In the recent past, as drought has worsened on western lands, the agency has devoted an increasingly significant portion of its resources to fighting fires.

Agency-wide, roughly 38,000 employees oversee 192.5 million acres. Although forestlands are concentrated in the West (87 percent of the agency acreage), the Forest Service manages more federal land in the East than all of the other federal agencies combined.

The National Forest System consists of 155 forests, 20 national grasslands, and an assortment of 121 other areas, all of which are organized into nine geographic regions, each with a regional forester at the helm. Forests comprise 188 million acres, 97.6 percent of the system. Each forest is directed by a supervisor who oversees ranger

U.S. Department of Agriculture
Forest Service

Forest Service
★ Chief

Field Administrative Units

- National Forest Regions (9)
  - ★ Regional Forester
- National Forests (155)
  - ★ Forest Supervisor
- Ranger Districts (630)
  - ★ District Ranger
- National Grasslands (20)
- Forest and Range
  - Experiment Stations (8)

Research

- Forest Environment
- Forest Inventory, Economics, and Recreation
- Forest Fire and Atmospheric Sciences
- Forest Insect and Disease
- Forest Products and Harvesting
- International Forestry
- Timber Management

National Forest System

- Ecosystem Management
- Engineering
- Minerals and Geology Management
- Forest Management
- Lands Management
- National Partnership Office
- Rangelands
- Recreation, Heritage and Wilderness
- Watershed and Air Management
- Wildlife and Fish and Rare Plants

State and Private Forestry

- Conservation Education
- Cooperative Forestry
- Fire and Aviation Management
- Forest Health Management
- Office of Tribal Relations
- Urban and Community Forestry

districts, the ground-level administrative units that perform daily forest management.

NATIONAL FOREST SYSTEM MANAGEMENT
Each of the multiple uses recognized by the MUSYA, with the addition of designated forest Wilderness, has its own management history and a set of challenges and conflicts. Brief descriptions of the major uses and some of the associated issues follow.

New Deal agencies like the Civilian Conservation Corps were instrumental in improving and popularizing public recreation areas in the United States.

Outdoor Recreation

Initially, the National Park Service was thought to be the agency charged with providing recreation opportunities on public land. In the 1920s and '30s, however, outdoor recreational use of both forests and parks increased as more people acquired automobiles. During the Great Depression, job programs such as the Civilian Conservation Corps built recreation facilities in many parks and forests, encouraging people to visit public lands. After World War II, American GIs returned home and the public turned more than ever to the outdoors for recreation. By the 1950s, the tremendous increase in recreational use had caused the deterioration of many facilities built in the 1930s. In national forest Wilderness areas, use increased by 700 percent between 1946 and 1964, and another 150 percent from the passage of the Wilderness Act in 1964 to 1989. Although Wilderness use leveled off in the 1980s, demand for a broad spectrum of recreational activities, including off-road-vehicle use and campgrounds, continued to increase.

In 2002, more than 214 million people visited Forest Service land, eighteen times the number of visitors in 1946. In particular, the use of off-highway vehicles (OHVs) has surged in popularity. OHVs in national forests grew in number from 5 million in 1972 to almost 36 million in 2000, and OHV users now account for 5 percent of the visits to national forests.[82] The ski industry is also a dominant player in the agency's recreation program, with more than 60 percent of the downhill skiing in the United States occurring in national forests.

Other than for downhill skiing, most recreational access to forests is unstructured, with numerous trailheads having no entrance stations, and therefore visitation is difficult to track with accuracy. It is clear, however, that visitation continues to rise and that recreation in national forests now far outpaces timber, mining, and grazing as the major source of economic impact on local economies adjacent to forestlands. Many people visit national forests, on their own or in groups, for day trips or self-guided overnight stays. Others choose to travel with the guidance of an outfitter or educational organization.

According to Forest Service regulation, most outfitted trips, even those operated by nonprofit organizations, are considered commercial activity. Service providers must secure official Special Use Permits to operate in the forests, and each permit carries stipulations that set a maximum allocation of use days and place restrictions on how and where an outfitter operates. Through the permit system, the Forest Service seeks to manage recreation with the intent of balancing use while minimizing risk to participants and impact on the land.

With the marked growth in recreation, both in number of visits and types of uses, the agency faces increasing challenges to provide opportunities to visitors while simultaneously protecting the resource.

Range

The Forest Service has managed rangelands since its inception in 1905. Debate over whether to allow grazing on forest reserves was one of the earliest and most contentious issues the agency faced. When he was chief, Gifford Pinchot argued that grazing should be controlled and carefully managed, but not prohibited.

A 2003 agency report shows that more than 95 million acres of forest system land—nearly half of the agency's total—in thirty-four states are available to grazing. The agency administers approximately 7,700 livestock permits totaling 9.6 million animal unit months (the unit of measurement for rangeland use) of grazing by cattle, horses, sheep, and goats.[83] The vast majority of this activity occurs on forest system land in the western states.

Timber

A policy of sustained yield was established in the early years of the Forest Service, and the agency engaged in a custodial timber practice until World War II. Gifford Pinchot and the foresters who followed him believed strongly in cutting at a rate not to exceed the rate of new growth. With the war, however, came a marked increase in the demand for timber. Instead of cutting sustainably, the Forest Service became a production-oriented agency. Following the war, the demand for timber continued to increase, and the agency continued to bolster its production. Timber harvest increased from an annual average of 1 billion board feet prior to the war to more than 12 billion by 1966. In support of this growth, road construction also increased dramatically.

In recent years, timber sales have declined by 80 percent, from an average of 12 billion board feet a year through the 1980s to just under 2 billion today. Emphasis has shifted from timber as a primary purpose of forests to a management regime more consistent with multiple use.

Watershed

The original forest reserves were founded with a concern for watershed protection. Intensive deforestation by the mid-nineteenth century had damaged watersheds, causing floods and decreased water quality and quantity. With the headwaters of most of the West's principal drainages located on national forests, water has been a critical concern of a wide variety of urban, agricultural, and mining interests over the years. Pinchot, along with succeeding chiefs, placed a high priority on protecting watersheds through timber practices designed for that purpose. Control over water, however, has traditionally been the responsibility of state governments.

Watershed protection remains a critical function of the national forest system today, particularly as the nation continues to increase its demand for water. Underscoring this purpose are the pressures on water supply created by persistent drought in many parts of the West in recent years.

Wildlife and Fish

Maintaining a sustainable yield of timber guided early Forest Service policy, with only incidental regard for wildlife. Pinchot's principal wildlife program involved predator control to protect livestock grazing. The agency created a Division of Wildlife in 1936, but wildlife management remained a low priority with the shift to intensive timber production during World War II.

In 1960, the enactment of the MUSYA elevated the status of wildlife and fish as legitimate uses of national forests, giving their management a boost in priority. The development of the science of ecology began to provide greater understanding of the role of wildlife in natural systems. Primary management responsibility, however, remained with the states. The MUSYA supported the system of cooperation between the agency and state wildlife programs by stating, "Nothing herein shall be construed as affecting the jurisdiction or responsibilities of the several states with respect to wildlife and fish on national forests."[84]

While protecting livestock from predators remains at the forefront for some western forests today, the agency's work on wildlife has taken on a much broader mission that includes species protection and management, habitat conservation, and scientific study.

Wilderness

The Forest Service is the agency credited with giving birth to the nation's first protected areas. In the early 1920s, Aldo Leopold lobbied for the preservation of 574,000 acres of the Gila National Forest as wilderness. It was with the passage of the Wilderness Act of 1964 that Wilderness became a critical component of the agency's multiple-use mandate.

Minerals

The U.S. Mining Law of 1872 allows access to all mineral deposits, such as gold, silver, copper, and other hard rocks, under national forests and grasslands. Other minerals, such as coal, potassium, sodium, phosphate, sand, gravel, oil, and gas, are regulated under the Mineral Leasing Act of 1920 and the Materials Act of 1947. An assortment of subsequent statutes has modified the earlier mining laws to change the way the activity can occur or prohibit it altogether. For example, the Wilderness Act of 1964 prohibited the staking of mining claims after January 1, 1984. Claims staked before that date may be developed if the natural character of the wilderness is maintained.

The Forest Service and BLM share responsibility for oil and gas development. The Federal Onshore Oil and Gas Leasing Reform Act of 1987 established the Forest Service as the lead agency for surface activities and environmental effects related to oil and gas exploration and development on national forests and grasslands. The BLM manages the subsurface activities, including the public lease sales through which developers gain access to public lands, even on national forests, to withdraw the minerals.

LAND USE PLANNING

The Forest Service is required by law to prepare and implement land use plans that guide the future of each forest. The Forest and Rangelands Renewable Resources Planning Act of 1974 (RPA), Federal Land Policy and Management Act of 1976 (FLPMA), and National Forest Management Act of 1976 (NFMA) direct the agency to evaluate the resource base of the forests—wildlife, recreation opportunities, mineral potential, timber, and so on—and implement a management approach that will serve the current and projected future demands of the public. Historically, the National Environmental Policy Act of 1969 (NEPA) required the agency to complete environmental impact statements for significant land use decisions, including the public in the formation of these decisions. This meant that the preparation of a forest plan included the completion of an EIS, providing the public with an opportunity to engage in the planning process.

As agency priorities shift over time, however, so does the act of long-range planning in the Forest Service. In 1999, President Clinton's administration proposed changes to the planning regulations to increase the agency's emphasis on ecological sustainability. In 2002, the Bush administration supplanted the Clinton regulations before they were implemented by proposing changes seeking to balance ecological sustainability with economic and social considerations. The new regulations, finalized in 2004, are designed to streamline the planning process by, among other things, removing the requirement to complete an EIS for each forest plan. Opponents of the new regulations expect them to reduce national direction in Forest Service planning and decrease the opportunity for public involvement.

The year 2005 marked the one hundredth anniversary of the Forest Service and began with a weeklong centennial forum and celebration in Washington, D.C., organized by the agency. The event brought together past agency chiefs, elected officials, department secretaries, partner organizations, and others to look back at the first hundred years and forward to the next century in the context of existing management challenges and opportunities. Forest Service Chief Dale Bosworth addressed the crowd with these words:

> In the one-hundred-year history of the Forest Service, the focus of management practices has changed with the times. In our early history, we were in a custodial period of management. Then,

during the Depression and World War II, we moved into a period where we had a lot of social responsibility. Recently, we were in an era of timber management and timber harvesting. But now it's my belief that we are in an era of restoration and recreation. We've built our communities and cities from the products of the national forests, and now it is time to reinvest and restore some of those forests.[85]

8

National Parks

NATIONAL PARK SERVICE

Established:	1916 by the National Park Service Organic Act
Administering agency:	U.S. Department of the Interior
Responsibility:	National parks, monuments, and other units
Total acreage:	84.4 million acres
Wilderness:	43.6 million acres
Budget (FY 2004):	$2.3 billion[86]
Employees (FY 2005):	20,399[87]
Website:	www.nps.gov
Mission:	Preservation and enjoyment of national parks and monuments

The National Park Service manages what are often referred to as the crown jewels of America's natural and cultural heritage. These jewels are surprisingly diverse, ranging from the Statue of Liberty National Monument to Yellowstone National Park, from the 13-million-acre Wrangell-St. Elias National Park and Preserve in Alaska to the .02-acre Thaddeus Kosciuszko National Memorial in Pennsylvania. The differences among these areas

TOM BOL

reflect the broad and sometimes uncertain mission of the agency, the roots of which can be attributed to the personalities that provided impassioned leadership in the first decades of service.

HISTORY OF THE NATIONAL PARK SERVICE

By the 1870s, exploitation and commercialization of America's magnificent natural areas led some to believe that these places were being mistreated. The wonders of Yellowstone captured the attention of the public and of Congress, leading to the passage of the Yellowstone Park Act of 1872. This act represented the first time that any nation had elected to preserve such a large area of undeveloped public land—roughly 2 million acres—from settlement or development and make it available for people to enjoy. It also introduced the concept of setting aside public land for the purpose of conservation and serves as a foundation for the agency's philosophy today.

After Yellowstone was created, growth in the NPS system came in fits and starts. In 1890, Congress authorized Yosemite, Sequoia, and General Grant National Parks (General Grant later merged with King's Canyon National Park). Crater Lake and Wind Cave National Parks were established in 1902 and 1903. The pace of new additions quickened when Congress became concerned about vandalism of Anasazi artifacts in the Southwest. By passing the Antiquities Act in 1906, Congress gave the chief executive authority to create national monuments by presidential proclamation, bypassing Congress, to protect cultural resources on lands already under federal jurisdiction. Theodore Roosevelt, and many who followed him, took advantage of this streamlined approach to protecting resources. By 1916, the nation had twenty national monuments.

A controversy at the turn of the century made clear the need for more structured control and management policies for national parks and monuments. The city of San Francisco, eyeing the waters of Yosemite's Tuolumne River to meet the needs of its growing population, chose the Hetch Hetchy valley as the best site for a dam. Debate over this project continued for more than a decade, with John Muir arguing for the protection of the remarkable natural and nonutilitarian values of the valley. The debate and the fate of the valley were settled when Congress passed legislation authorizing the dam in 1913. Although the decision was a great loss for those who viewed parks as precious reserves that should be immune to development pressures, the incident spawned intense national debate, resulting in greater public scrutiny of park management practices.

The scrutiny led Congress to impose legislative structure to encourage better management of the growing number of parks and monuments. Structure came in the form of the National Park Service Organic Act of 1916. The act formally established the agency and its mission in the following statement:

> The service thus established shall promote and regulate the use of the Federal areas known as national parks, monuments, and reservations . . . by such means and measures as conform to the fundamental purpose of the said parks, monuments and reservations, which purpose is to conserve the scenery and the natural and historic objects and the wild life therein and to provide for the enjoyment of the same in such a manner and by such means as will leave them unimpaired for the enjoyment of future generations.[88]

The act established for the NPS a dual mission: "to conserve" and "to provide for the enjoyment" of park resources. Over the years, many have considered this dual mission contradictory, leading to policies and regulations that conflict, and disagreements between the public and the political system about park priorities. The agency continually struggles—even today—to be responsive to both those who call for additional developed recreation facilities and those who support greater attention to preserving natural park values.

With its mission laid out in statute, the NPS forged ahead with Stephen Mather as its first director. No one person or piece of legislation did more to define the management and popular conception of the agency than Mather, who stayed at the helm of the Park Service for thirteen years. Mather was driven by a vision of the exalted place that he believed national parks should occupy in American culture. He used his skill as a promoter and a substantial amount of his personal wealth to promote the grandeur of the parks in the parlors of the nation.

To build support for the parks, Mather focused on providing access to them, since most were far away from the population centers of the East, remote, and inaccessible. He first struck deals with the railroads to run lines to park boundaries, and then built comfortable accommodations so that visitors could make a "civilized" trip to the wilds of Grand Canyon or Glacier National Park. Once automobiles entered the social scene, Mather urged the construction of motorways to increase access. To garner the support of easterners for the idea of national parks, Mather encouraged the designation of Great Smoky Mountains and Shenandoah National Parks. Congress authorized both in 1926.

Horace Albright replaced Mather and directed the NPS from 1929 to 1933. He oversaw the addition of a large number of sites previously managed by the Forest Service and War Department. A 1933 Executive Order transferred to the Park Service authority to manage all national memorials, monuments, battlefields, and an assortment of other historic sites. Albright also expanded the educational function of the NPS by developing interpretive programs and museums within parks.

For the half century kicked off by Mather and Albright, the NPS pursued its preservationist mission by focusing primarily on accommodating visitors, building hotels and tourist facilities, and eradicating so-called "bad" animals (predators). In the 1930s, George Wright initiated a movement to integrate science into the development of park policy. When Wright was killed in a car accident, the effort stalled for another thirty years. As a result, for decades the NPS lacked a strong commitment to science-based stewardship, leaving it vulnerable to charges of mismanagement.

Poaching also had a significant effect on the management direction of the NPS. It occurred rather freely during the early years at Yellowstone National Park. A park-sanctioned expedition to Yellowstone by the state of California to collect bears—the state symbol—ended in a debacle that caused an uproar over park management.

Finally, in the 1960s, after the public reacted with horror to the shooting of elk by NPS representatives in Yellowstone, the secretary of the interior appointed a committee of scientists, under the direction of Starker Leopold (Aldo Leopold's oldest son), to provide advice on the park's elk population problem. The group released the Leopold Report, a document that fundamentally shifted the agency's view of its management role and set into motion the ongoing debate over the Park Service's approach to preservation. The report made a powerful case for revising the agency's resource management policies, as summarized in this statement: "As a primary goal, we would recommend that the biotic associations within each park be maintained, or where necessary recreated, as nearly as possible in the condition that prevailed when the area was first visited by the white man. A national park should represent a vignette of primitive America."[89]

Following publication of the report, Secretary of the Interior Stewart Udall required the parks to manage natural areas to maintain and reestablish indigenous plant and animal life. Preservation policy was revised in response, and the agency implemented controversial non-intervention and restoration policies, based on the premise that human interference with ecological processes should be avoided generally or corrected where necessary to restore a functioning ecological complex.

Due in large part to the Leopold Report, the NPS now defines its statutory preservation responsibilities in terms of maintaining and restoring native species and processes while minimizing human intervention with natural ecosystem processes. Many have criticized this approach as unattainable and biocentric, ignoring the importance of human presence in nature. Persistent disagreements have left the preservation policy vulnerable, in spite of being grounded in legal mandate. The science that supports the preservation policy is not fully accepted, and parks struggle to coexist with neighboring landowners and visitors who may have different opinions about how public land should be managed. As demonstrated in places like the Grand Canyon and Yellowstone, "the greatest risk to the [preservation] policy is its incremental or piecemeal erosion in the face of local political pressure and scientific criticism."[90]

ORGANIZATION

Headquartered in Washington, D.C., the National Park Service is housed in the Department of the Interior. Reporting to the secretary, seven regional agency offices oversee the park system, which includes 388 units on 84.4 million acres. Each park unit is led by a superintendent. These units include a surprisingly long list of different designations. Aside from the fifty-eight national parks, the agency manages historic sites, monuments, battlefields, capitol parks, recreation areas, military parks, historic parks, scenic rivers and trails, seashores, lakeshores, memorials, parkways, preserves, the National Mall, and the White House.

NATIONAL PARK SYSTEM MANAGEMENT

In a nutshell, the mission of the National Park Service is to preserve and protect the resources under its care while allowing for recreation. The tremendous variety of units

amplifies the obvious conflicts that this mission introduces. The NPS manages Ford's Theatre in downtown
Washington, D.C., as well as Denali National Park in the
rugged and remote Alaska Range. Clearly, one management prescription does not serve all units equally well,
and park managers must be closely in touch with the
unique qualities and characteristics of the areas under
their care.

In general, activities that extract natural resources,
such as timber, oil and gas, and hardrock mining, are not
permitted inside national parks, though in some cases
specific legislation allows for such uses. Many national
parks and monuments employ a zoning scheme that
determines what activities are appropriate for different
regions within their boundaries. A brief outline of the
zones sheds light on how the agency makes on-the-
ground decisions that reflect its dual mission.

Natural Zone

The natural zone is managed to maintain the primitive
character and natural processes within the area. Natural
zones may contain Wilderness subzones. Currently, 53
percent of the national park system (44 million acres) has
been designated Wilderness by Congress.[91] Another 31
percent of NPS acres have been recommended as either
Wilderness or study areas to be further evaluated as
potential Wilderness. Land that is suitable for study or
has been proposed is managed as de facto Wilderness to
preserve its natural character until Congress determines
the final classification.

Cultural Zone

Management strategies in the cultural zone focus on protection, interpretation, and selective restoration of historic
and archaeological resources.

U.S. Department of the Interior

National Park Service

Director

Comptroller	Deputy Director Operations	Deputy Director Support Services
Accounting	U.S. Park Police	American Indian Liason
Budget	Assistant Director Business Services	International Affairs
	Assistant Director Human Capital	Chief Information Officer
	Associate Director Cultural Resources	Policy
	Associate Director Natural Resources, Stewardship, and Science	Strategic Planning
	Associate Director Visitor and Resource Protection	State and Local Assistance Programs
	Associate Director Park Planning, Facilities, and Lands	Special Projects and Initiatives
	Associate Director Partnerships, Interpretation and Education, Volunteers, and Outdoor Recreation	
	Regional Directors	

Park Superintendents

Development Zone
The development zone provides areas for visitor and administrative facilities, such as visitor centers, developed campgrounds, road corridors, and maintenance yards.

Recreation Management
Initially, the NPS was thought to be the primary provider of recreation opportunities for the American public.

Stephen Mather set the pace, equipping the parks to host visitors by building large hotels and visitor centers and paving the way, literally, for transportation to park entrances. Unlike the Forest Service, the park system has entrance stations through which all visitors pass, allowing the NPS to track with relative accuracy the number of people who visit its parks each year. The historical trend in park visitation tells the story of its growth. In 1940, 21 million people visited national parks. The NPS placed attracting visitors high on its priority list, and by 1970, that number had grown to 172 million. With the burgeoning popularity of recreation and tourism, the number swelled to 421 million by 2002.[92]

As does the Forest Service, the NPS manages organized recreation—guided visits or trips—through a permit system. Each park superintendent is responsible for determining what activities and services are appropriate. To operate inside a park, services such as hotels, food purveyors, and others that require capital investment in buildings or other infrastructure are required to have a concession contract. Receiving a concession is a fairly elaborate competitive process by which the park issues a prospectus, announcing the need for a service, and interested providers respond with a proposal, including a financial bid. After analyzing the proposals, the park selects which one will provide the service.

Outfitters, guides, and other service providers that don't make capital improvements within the parks currently operate under the incidental business permit (IBP) system. Like the special use permit in the Forest Service, the IBP is an agreement between the NPS and a provider of a service, most commonly an outfitter, outdoor educator, or T-shirt sales type of business. Establishing conditions under which the permittee may operate. It provides the agency with the ability to place restrictions on how, when, where, and how much a service will be provided. Partly in response to increased visitation and the growth in popularity of recreation in the parks, the agency is now in the process of redesigning the nonconcession commercial permit system to create commercial use authorizations. This will enable parks to limit the number of permits they offer to outside service providers, thus introducing an element of competition in the provision of commercial services in national parks.

LAND USE PLANNING

Under mandate of the Organic Act, each operating unit of the NPS maintains a general management plan (GMP), the purpose of which is to ensure that each park has a clearly defined direction for resource preservation and visitor use. Multiple action plans pertaining to specific aspects of park management, such as travel or commercial use, tier from the GMP. Park planning determines what types of resource conditions, visitor uses, and management actions will best achieve the agency's mission. The basic foundation for GMPs consists of analysis of existing and potential resource conditions and visitor experiences, assessment of environmental impacts, and costs of alternative courses of action. The National Environmental Policy Act provides a mechanism for the public to participate in the planning process, ensuring that the NPS understands and considers the public's interests in the parks.

9

Public Lands of the Bureau of Land Management

If one were to define and differentiate between national parks and national forests to a child, it would be fairly easy to do in a general way by describing the physical characteristics of the land. Parks are awe-inspiring places of dramatic beauty and wild character. Gazing at scenery within a park, we know why it was set aside as a park. National forests are generally, though not always, heavily forested mountains, hillsides, and river valleys, providing homes for wildlife and fish and sources of clean water and air. The bulk of public land acreage, however, falls into neither of these categories. These leftover federal lands were initially considered to hold minimal value, and the early U.S. government sought to sell them off to encourage development of the West.

Today stewardship of what are generally known as the public lands is the charge of the Bureau of Land Management, created in 1946 by the merger of the General Land Office and the U.S. Grazing Service. The questions of which public lands to retain and how to manage them were at the heart of debate for two centuries. The history of the BLM reflects this debate.

HISTORY OF THE BUREAU OF LAND MANAGEMENT

The roots of the BLM lie in the General Land Office, the federal government's office of real estate, created to oversee the disposal of the public lands acquired from foreign countries that comprised the Lower 48 states, excluding the area of the original thirteen colonies. Until 1934, the General Land Office divided public lands into the hands of private landowners under the guidance of the Homestead Act of 1862. By the 1930s, much of the land had been given away, resulting in a checkerboard pattern of federal and private ownership across much of the western United States. The unsold lands remaining in federal hands were considered the "leftover" lands—apparently no one wanted them.

President Franklin Roosevelt's administration set the groundwork for the modern management of these leftover lands. With Secretary of the Interior Harold Ickes, he created a plan to manage the remaining public lands for the public good. No longer would lands outside of the national forest and park systems be given away. Instead, they would be managed according to conservation principles so that use, principally grazing, could continue in an orderly manner.

The Taylor Grazing Act of 1934, championed by Ickes, established in law the principle that the remaining public lands would be managed by the government for good purpose. The act created the U.S. Grazing Service to manage lands suitable for grazing that were otherwise administered by the General Land Office. The act states the purpose of the service:

> In order to promote the highest use of the public lands pending its final disposal, the Secretary of the Interior is authorized . . . to establish grazing districts or additions thereto and/or modify the boundaries thereof, of vacant, unappropriated, and unreserved lands from any part of the public domain of the United States (exclusive of Alaska), which are not in national forests, national parks and monuments, Indian reservations . . . and which in his opinion are chiefly valuable for grazing and raising forage crops.
>
> The Secretary of the Interior shall make provision for the protection, administration, regulation, and improvement of such grazing districts . . . and to insure the objects of such grazing districts, namely, to regulate their occupancy and use, to preserve the land and its resources from destruction or unnecessary injury, to provide for the orderly use, improvement, and development of the range.[95]

Oddly enough, the words "pending its final disposal" indicate that the Taylor Grazing Act left the door open for the federal government to sell these lands, in spite of the founding intent of the legislation. It would still take some time for Congress to legislate that the retention of these lands would serve the national interest.

For the next decade, the Grazing Service limped from one controversy to the next. New grazing fees were unwelcome, and ranchers tried successfully to intimidate the service. Sen. Pat McCarran from Nevada represented the grazing interests in Congress and was successful in causing appropriations for the service to dwindle. The service's budget dropped to such a low level that it was barely able to enforce regulations or even manage daily functions. Ranchers exercised unabashed influence by contributing part of the budget. In 1947, more than 40 percent of appropriations was provided by ranchers who funneled money through the advisory boards established by the Taylor Grazing Act. This tended to put the Grazing Service in an awkward situation.

In 1946, President Harry Truman oversaw elimination of the Grazing Service by merging it with the General Land Office and creating a new agency called the Bureau of Land Management. Created through administrative reorganization based on presidential authority, the BLM had no statutory foundation. This lack of statutory authority, combined with the myriad laws governing public land management, led Congress to institute the Public Land Law Review Commission (PLLRC), charged with reviewing public land laws and regulations to determine what, if any, revisions were necessary to ensure their compatibility and fit with the future needs of the country.

In 1970, the PLLRC completed a report titled *One Third of the Nation's Land*, which offered 137 recommendations for more efficient and effective management of 755 million acres of public land. Congress eventually acted on the recommendations that identified the BLM's need for statutory authority. Within six years, authority came in the form of the Federal Land Policy and Management Act of 1976. In addition to giving the agency a legal foundation, the law laid down the fundamental principles for future federal land management and officially declared the BLM's days of disposal over. The opening sections of the act make broad policy statements:

> The Congress declares that it is the policy of the United States that:
>
> the public lands be retained in Federal ownership, unless as a result of the land use planning procedure provided for in this Act, it is determined that disposal of a particular parcel will serve the national interest;
>
> the national interest will be best realized if the public lands and their resources are periodically and systematically inventoried and their present and future use is projected through a land use planning process coordinated with other Federal and State planning efforts;
>
> . . . management be on the basis of multiple use and sustained yield unless otherwise specified by law;
>
> the public lands be managed in a manner that will protect the quality of scientific, scenic, historical, ecological, environmental, air and atmosphere, water resources, and archaeological values; that, where appropriate, will preserve and protect certain public lands in their natural condition; that will provide food and habitat for fish and wildlife

and domestic animals; and that will provide for outdoor recreation and human occupancy and use;

the United States will receive fair market value of the use of the public lands and their resources unless otherwise provided for by statute . . . ;

. . . regulations and plans for the protection of public land areas of critical environmental concern be promptly developed.[96]

The enactment of FLPMA brought to rest the longstanding debate over the disposal or retention of public land. Land would be retained and managed for the public good. But public-land policy is rarely issue-free, and this shift in approach spawned the "sagebrush rebellion" in the late 1970s and early 1980s, a movement led by westerners who resented the federal presence in their states and wanted the government to maintain its original policy of transferring landownership to private and state hands. Decades later, this local-federal tension continues to be a significant hurdle in making land use decisions and establishing long-term land management plans.

By adding Wilderness and a broader base of other uses to the BLM's mandate, FLPMA created a larger and more diverse constituency for BLM land. No longer beholden to the specific interests of one group—the livestock-grazing permit holders—the agency could call on the support of Wilderness proponents, primitive recreation enthusiasts, and many others with an interest in the future of what was once considered leftover land.

FLPMA ended the debate about land disposal and firmly established in the BLM the principles of multiple use and sustained yield—the same guiding principles followed by the Forest Service. But in broadening the base of possible uses for the land, the act also set the stage for the primary challenge the BLM now faces: how to determine the best use of the land in its care. FLPMA also sent the BLM scrambling for staff members who knew something about recreation, Wilderness, and other uses defined by the multiple-use mission.

ORGANIZATION

The BLM administers more federal land than any other agency—262 million acres (nearly 12 percent of all the land in the country), most of which is located in the western United States. One-third of the acreage is in Alaska. Like the National Park Service and Fish and Wildlife Service, the BLM is a division of the Department of the Interior, with its headquarters located in Washington, D.C.

The agency is led by a director, a political appointee who reports to the secretary of the interior through the assistant secretary for land and minerals management. The director oversees twelve state offices, each managed by a state director and administering a specific geographic area, mostly conforming to state boundaries. These are divided into field offices, which implement BLM programs and policies on the ground.

BLM MANAGEMENT

It is surprising to think that BLM lands were long considered leftovers when you understand their breadth, variety, and beauty. From the sweeping reaches of the Owyhee River in southeast Oregon to the striking red-rock canyons of Utah, to the sublime peace of the Red Desert in Wyoming, these lands are as much a national treasure as other federal land. They include rolling prairie, arctic tundra, forest, and desert. They hold a diverse array of resources, including timber, minerals and fuels, forage, wild horses and burros, fish and wildlife habitat, recreation sites, Wilderness, archaeological and historical sites, and natural heritage resources. In addition, the agency manages 700 million acres of federal subsurface mineral resources and supervises the mineral operations on 56 million acres of Indian trust lands.[97] The BLM is also responsible for fire suppression on 370 million acres of Interior Department and other federal land, as well as some nonfederal land. Three major areas define the BLM's substantial management responsibilities: rangelands, energy and minerals, and the National Landscape Conservation System (NLCS).

Rangelands

BLM management is firmly grounded in livestock grazing, as defined originally by the Taylor Grazing Act, which established a system of exclusive permits to graze allotted areas of land. Following Taylor, FLPMA set overall land management objectives. Close on the heels of FLPMA, the Public Rangelands Improvement Act of 1978 acknowledged continuing concern over the condition of public rangelands and mandated more specific resource management requirements for the BLM.

In 2004, ranchers held permits to graze livestock on 162 million of the agency's 262 million acres (62 percent of BLM land). Permit fees for livestock grazing are based on the animal unit month (AUM), the amount of forage a mature cow or five sheep consumes in one month. In 1990, the fee per AUM was $1.81; in 2004, $1.43. According to a 2004 congressional research report, roughly 4.5 percent of the BLM's revenue is derived from grazing activity.[98]

Rangelands also provide forage for wildlife and wild horses and burros. The Wild, Free-Roaming Horses and Burros Act of 1971 protects these animals on federal land. In 2004, about 60,000 wild horses and burros were under BLM management—36,000 on open range and 24,000 in holding facilities.[99] The agency believes that this herd size is too large to be sustainable and is attempting to reduce it through adoption, fertility control, and holding programs. Insufficient funding has hampered the agency's ability to manage wild horses and burros properly, aggravating the conflict and controversy that have surrounded this issue for years.

Energy and Minerals

The BLM has management authority over energy and mineral development on 700 million acres of federal land and serves three basic functions in this area: It holds competitive and noncompetitive leases for oil, gas, geothermal steam, potash, coal, and other minerals; assists in locating and issuing patents of hard-rock minerals, such as gold, silver, uranium, copper, and molybdenum; and sells construction-grade materials, such as sand, gravel, clay, and stone.

Roughly 165 million acres of the 700 million, including most of the national park system and the National Wilderness Preservation System, have been withdrawn from mineral leasing and sale, except for valid existing rights within those areas. Mineral development on an additional 182 million acres is subject to the approval of the surface management agency. For example, the Forest Service must approve the leasing of land for mineral development within national forests; the BLM manages any leasing that is approved.

In 2003, 42 percent of the coal, 11 percent of the natural gas, and 5 percent of the oil produced in the United States came from BLM-managed lands. Total revenues earned from the sale of these resources amounted to $2.2 billion, 50 percent of which was shared with the states in which the land is located (90 percent with Alaska).[100] The demand for energy resources from BLM land continues to grow as the federal government strives to increase domestic energy production in response to high rates of U.S. consumption and war in the Middle East.

National Landscape Conservation System

In 2000, the BLM created the NLCS to give more management attention and resources to the national monuments, conservation areas, Wilderness areas and study areas, wild and scenic rivers, and historic trails within its care. The system currently totals 42 million acres, excluding trails and rivers, and includes fifteen monuments and seventeen national conservation areas.[101] The BLM's NLCS management emphasis is resource conservation to serve recreation. Other activities can occur if they are compatible with the designation.

Recreation Management

As the popularity of outdoor recreation activities in the United States has grown, and urban areas have sprawled toward public-land borders, especially in the West, recreation management has become an increasingly important part of the BLM's multiple-use mission. Recreation activities on BLM land cover the full spectrum, including hunting, fishing, visiting cultural and historic sites, birdwatching, hiking, picnicking, camping, boating, mountain biking, and off-highway vehicle use. Similarly to the Forest Service and Park Service, the BLM requires that providers of recreation services, such as outfitters and guides, obtain commercial permits and pay fees to use the public lands to support their businesses. At 394 BLM recreation sites, visitors pay fees authorized by the national Recreation Fee Demonstration Program, a controversial effort to help subsidize agency recreation budgets.[102]

The increase of recreational activities on BLM land has added to the inherent challenge of balancing a long list of uses and demands. In 1998, the BLM reported 50 million visits. By 2004, that number had grown to 66.6 million.[103] Recreation at times conflicts with commodity-driven uses, such as oil and gas development, and conflicts also arise within the recreation community when one group objects to another's utilization of BLM land.

LAND USE PLANNING

All BLM lands, including the mineral estate, are managed in accordance with land use plans developed by the agency. Many plans currently in place date back to the 1970s and '80s, when the agency first initiated planning efforts in response to FLPMA. Aging plans are now exacerbating many of the use conflicts. The agency lacks current data, information, and plans to support decisions regarding new uses, issues, and changed circumstances. In 2001, the BLM began a multiyear effort to revise existing resource management plans. This effort is made more urgent by such societal changes as greater demand for access to energy resources, largely oil and gas; an increase in the use of off-highway vehicles; and a need to address growing concerns about the effects of wildfire.

10

National Refuges

Established:	1956 by the Fish and Wildlife Act
Administering agency:	U.S. Fish and Wildlife Service, Department of the Interior
Responsibility:	National Wildlife Refuge System, migratory birds, endangered species, marine mammals, freshwater and anadromous fish
Total acreage:	95.4 million acres
Wilderness:	20.7 million acres
Budget (FY 2004):	$1.3 billion[104]
Employees (FY 2004):	9,345[105]
Website:	www.fws.gov
Mission:	Working with others to conserve, protect, and enhance fish, wildlife, and plants and their habitats for the continuing benefit of the American people

By virtue of its name, the U.S. Fish and Wildlife Service (FWS) would seem to have a particularly focused mission. Unlike the other three federal agencies, which have broad responsibility for a category of land, the mandate of the FWS is to preserve and restore designated lands and waters to provide for wildlife. Other uses, such as hunting, fishing, recreation, grazing, and oil and gas development, are permitted only if determined to be compatible with the primary purpose. This focus took some time to develop, however, and for many years, the agency lacked legal authority to support its management actions. Recent legislation has enabled the FWS to sharpen its focus on fish and wildlife, helping to resolve ambiguity in its mission. Today the National Wildlife Refuge System stands for many as an international model of resource management and protection.

HISTORY OF THE NATIONAL WILDLIFE REFUGE SYSTEM

Like the NPS, Forest Service, and BLM, the roots of the National Wildlife Refuge System and its parent agency, the FWS, can be traced back to the late 1800s. The modern FWS is heir to two primary lineages: a federal agency responsible for fisheries, and another for studying and protecting selected birds and mammals.

The fishery lineage began in the 1860s, when a decline in fish catches prompted Congress to establish a commission to study the problem and suggest improvements in fishery practices. In 1871, Congress created the U.S. Fish Commission. An internal reorganization in 1903 placed the commission in the Department of Commerce and renamed it the Bureau of Fisheries.

In 1885, Congress established the Office of Economic Ornithology in the Department of Agriculture to study migratory birds and determine their effects on agriculture along the major flyways. By 1905, the Office of Economic Ornithology expanded its responsibilities to become the

Bureau of Biological Survey, the purpose of which was to study the abundance, distribution, and habits of birds and mammals. The bureau, which was similar to the modern FWS, managed the nation's first refuges, enforced wildlife laws, controlled predators, and conserved endangered wildlife populations.

Compatibility of purpose between the Bureaus of Fisheries and Biological Survey prompted Congress to combine the two agencies in 1940. Legislation created the Fish and Wildlife Service—not quite the current incarnation—and transferred the bureaus from the Agriculture and Commerce Departments to the Department of the Interior. In 1956, a final reorganization, as a result of the Fish and Wildlife Act, created the U.S. Fish and Wildlife Service as we know it today. Ten years later, the National Wildlife Refuge Administration Act established the National Wildlife Refuge System under the management of the FWS.

President Theodore Roosevelt established the first national wildlife refuge in 1903 at Pelican Island in Florida. Within six years, he declared a total of fifty-one bird and four big-game reserves. By 2003, the system totaled 540 refuges encompassing 92 million acres in fifty states, the Pacific Territories, Puerto Rico, and the Virgin Islands.[106] With the passage of the Alaska National Interest Lands Conservation Act (ANILCA) in 1980, the system gained its largest increase in acreage, adding 53 million acres. Close to 77 million acres of refuge lands—80 percent of the total system—are now located in Alaska.

ORGANIZATION

The FWS is headquartered in Washington, D.C., and housed in the Department of the Interior. A director leads the service and oversees a staff with responsibilities for the agency's major program areas: fishery resources, wildlife resources, habitat resources, research and development, and federal assistance to state programs. The wildlife resources program oversees the National Wildlife Refuge System (NWRS). Seven regional offices administer programs and coordinate between the field units and Washington.

In addition to refuges, the NWRS includes two other categories of protected land: waterfowl production areas (WPAs), private lands managed by agreements between the owners and the FWS to provide breeding habitat for migratory waterfowl; and wildlife coordination areas (WCAs), which are largely owned by the FWS but are managed by state agencies in agreement with FWS. Totaling WPAs, WCAs, and refuges brings the FWS unit count to 793 on 95.4 million acres.

FISH AND WILDLIFE SERVICE MANAGEMENT

The Fish and Wildlife Act of 1956 was critical in establishing the authority to create and acquire refuges. It did not, however, provide clear, systemic management guidance for the agency. Lacking this legislative guidance, the FWS struggled for several decades to define the stewardship of fish and wildlife as its primary management priority. The agency suffered from poor funding and the influence of encroaching uses, such as recreation and mineral development, that were considered to be incompatible with healthy habitat for wildlife and fish. It wasn't until the 1960s, and then finally the late 1990s, that Congress passed additional legislation that helped set the agency on a clearer course for refuge management.

The Refuge Recreation Act of 1962 and National Wildlife Refuge System Improvement Act of 1997 filled the void in management guidance for the FWS, providing a system-wide basis for restricting or encouraging certain activities within refuges. The Recreation Act created a compatibility standard, which imposes certain restrictions on use and then provides a regulatory framework, such as a permit system, to allow otherwise prohibited activities. It has become the cornerstone of refuge management and the key tool for managers to determine which uses are appropriate within a given refuge. This concept was later incorporated into such landmark environmental legislation as the Clean Air Act, Clean Water Act, and amendments to the Endangered Species Act.

The agency's struggle to balance the desire to protect natural resources with the pressure to satisfy recreation and other needs culminated in the 1997 Refuge Improvement Act. This act weighs conservation heavily, mandating biological integrity, and employs the compatibility standard to find management balance. But it also established the importance of public use, required the agency to produce written analysis of compatibility, and mandated the development of comprehensive conservation plans for each unit in the system. Congress stated the purpose of the act as follows: "The mission of the system is to administer a national network of lands and waters for the conservation, management, and where appropriate, restoration of the fish, wildlife and plant resources and their habitats within the United States for the benefit of present and future generations of Americans."[107] An important provision of the law designated "compatible wildlife-dependent recreational uses involving hunting, fishing, wildlife observation and photography, and environmental education and interpretation as priority public uses of the Refuge System," and further defined that priority public uses must "receive enhanced consideration over other general public uses in planning and management within the System."[108]

In a paper evaluating the legislative history of the NWRS, Robert Fischman notes a critical difference between the FWS mission and that of its public land counterparts. Fischman states, "The framework adopted in the 1997 Act clearly elevates conservation above wildlife-dependent recreation and provides no recourse to wildlife-dependent recreationists who find their activities impaired by other types of wildlife-dependent recreation."[109]

The FWS Refuge Manual describes the agency's mission in the following terms:

To perpetuate the migratory bird resource.

To preserve a natural diversity and abundance of fauna and flora on refuge lands.

To preserve, restore and enhance in their natural ecosystems all species of animals and plants that are endangered or threatened with becoming endangered or threatened.

To provide an understanding and appreciation of fish and wildlife ecology and humans' role in their environment, and to provide refuge visitors with high-quality, safe, wholesome, and enjoyable recreational experiences oriented toward wildlife, to the extent these activities are compatible with the purpose for which the refuge was established.

Though wildlife, fish, and their habitat clearly gained the upper hand in refuge management, other uses may still be permitted, provided that they are compatible with wildlife. This has left the door open to continuing conflict over what uses are deemed to be compatible with the purpose of the system. The most infamous battle in recent years has been the controversy—still raging in 2005—over developing oil and gas reserves in the Arctic National Wildlife Refuge on the coastal plain of northern Alaska.

THE ENDANGERED SPECIES ACT

One of the primary objectives of the FWS is to enforce the provisions of the Endangered Species Act of 1973. The FWS, along with the National Marine Fisheries Service (NMFS), is responsible for determining what species are endangered and what lands or waters are critical to the recovery of those species.

The agency lists species as either endangered or threatened, depending on the severity of the species' situation. An endangered species is one determined to be on the brink of extinction; a threatened species is one that, without government intervention, will soon be endangered. Species outside the United States may be listed; for example, the giant panda and snow leopard are foreign species currently listed by the FWS.

LAND USE PLANNING

Until the 1980s and 1990s, when Congress finally passed a true organic act, or founding authority for the FWS, the agency was largely free from comprehensive system-wide planning requirements. This undoubtedly played a significant role in the struggles the agency faced to establish clear management actions. When Congress passed the Alaska National Interest Lands Conservation Act in 1980, the statute forced the agency to engage in comprehensive planning for the NWRS units located in that state. Planning experience with ANILCA set the stage for implementation of a system-wide planning requirement with the passage of the Refuge Improvement Act in 1997. Following the model established by the National Forest Management Act, the Improvement Act requires the FWS to prepare a comprehensive conservation plan for each unit within fifteen years and update each plan every fifteen years, or sooner if conditions change significantly.[110]

11

Special Management Systems on Federal Lands: Wilderness, Wild Rivers, and Scenic Trails

What a country chooses to save is what a country chooses to say about itself.

—Mollie Beatty

In addition to the four primary federal land management systems—national forests, national parks, national refuges, and public lands managed by the BLM—three additional special management systems include lands from all four agencies. These systems—the National Wilderness Preservation System, National Wild and Scenic Rivers System, and National Trails System—dictate an overall management goal, specified by statute, that over-rides what would otherwise be an agency-specific approach to management. The National Wilderness Preservation System has significant history and has been

TOM WRIGHT

the focus of a great deal of management attention and conflict. This chapter also more briefly introduces the other two systems, which are newer to public lands and less recognized by the public; for more details, explore the additional information sources provided in Appendix A.

THE NATIONAL WILDERNESS PRESERVATION SYSTEM

> *I hope that the United States of America is not so rich that she can afford to let these wildernesses pass by. Or so poor that she cannot afford to keep them.*
>
> —Mardy Murie

The National Wilderness Preservation System (NWPS) has no distinct managing agency, designated personnel, or appropriations specifically allocated for its manage-

Capital-"W" Wilderness areas fall under the jurisidiction of the National Wildlife Preservation System and can be found in almost every state.

ment. It is, however, a critical component of the nation's federal land heritage, including specially designated protected areas managed by all four federal agencies. The Wilderness Act of 1964 designated the Forest Service, National Park Service, and Fish and Wildlife Service as stewards of wilderness. In 1976, the Federal Land Policy and Management Act added the Bureau of Land Management to the NWPS.

Today the NWPS includes more than 105 million acres of wild country in 662 areas from nearly all regions of the nation.[111] This amounts to 4.7 percent of all land in the United States, and 16 percent of all federal land. Close to 44 million acres of congressionally designated Wilderness are located within national parks; 34.8 million in national forests; 20.7 million inside national refuges, managed by the FWS; and a scant 6.5 million of BLM land.[112] More than half of all Wilderness lies in the parks, refuges, and forests of Alaska; less than 5 percent is located in the East. All states hold some designated Wilderness, with the exception of six: Connecticut, Delaware, Iowa, Kansas, Maryland, and Rhode Island. Wilderness areas vary greatly in size. The smallest is the 5-acre Pelican Island National Wildlife Refuge off the coast of Florida, and the largest covers 9 million acres of Wrangell-St. Elias National Park in Alaska.

Legal Basis for Wilderness: The Wilderness Act of 1964

After years of debate, Congress passed the Wilderness Act in September 1964. The act defines for the American public an eloquent purpose for Wilderness, and its stirring language has provided a strong hold for the country's conservation movement. One of the most profound, oft-quoted, and critical concepts presented by the act lays out the significance of designated Wilderness:

> In order to assure that an increasing population, accompanied by expanding settlement and growing mechanization, does not occupy and modify all areas within the United States and its possessions, leaving no lands designated for preservation and protection in their natural condition, it is hereby declared to be the policy of the Congress to secure for the American people of present and future generations the benefits of an enduring resource of wilderness.[113]

With this language, the authors exhibit remarkable vision. They recognized, even in the 1950s, that the pace of development in the country would quicken, placing natural places at risk. The act suggests a higher purpose for Wilderness and an obligation for the country to exhibit some restraint in serving that purpose. In addition to establishing a purpose, the act provides a descriptive definition of Wilderness:

A wilderness, in contrast with those areas where man and his own works dominate the landscape, is hereby recognized as an area where the earth and its community of life are untrammeled by man, where man himself is a visitor who does not remain. An area of wilderness is further defined to mean in this Act an area of undeveloped Federal land retaining its primeval character and influence, without permanent improvements or habitation, which is protected and managed so as to preserve its natural conditions and which (1) generally appears to have been affected primarily by the forces of nature, with the imprint of man's work substantially unnoticeable; (2) has outstanding opportunities for solitude or a primitive and unconfined type of recreation; (3) has at least five thousand acres of land or is of sufficient size as to make practicable its preservation and use in an unimpaired condition; and (4) may also contain ecological, geological, or other features of scientific, educational, scenic, or historical value.[114]

The act charges the federal agencies with the task of managing Wilderness to preserve its natural character and mandates that it be devoted to the public purposes of recreational, scenic, scientific, educational, conservation, and historical use. The act prohibits certain uses, such as commercial enterprise, permanent roads, mechanized vehicles (including bicycles), and structures or installations, unless grandfathered for a prior purpose. Special provisions in the act allow mining on claims staked before 1983 and livestock grazing in areas where it was established prior to Wilderness designation. These provisions represent fundamental compromises in the act, without which it might never have become law.

In spite of relatively clear definition by the act, however, Wilderness has been and continues to be the topic of much debate and disagreement, stemming from differences in interpretation of the legislation's wording and the concerns of some that wilderness represents a lockup of public land.

The Process of Wilderness Designation

The Wilderness Act outlines three stages in the process by which federal land can be designated as Wilderness:

1. Classification. The agency reviews its holdings and recommends areas that it believes fit the character of Wilderness. These recommendations are sent to the secretary of the agency (either agriculture or the interior), who presents them to the president.
2. Presidential recommendation to Congress. The president transmits to Congress the recommendations provided by the agency, including maps and boundary definition for each unit of Wilderness proposed.
3. Approval. Congress must then pass a law that establishes a proposed Wilderness area as permanent. This is often a very political part of the process, because Congress can elect to follow the recommendations, ignore them entirely, or develop

a new proposal that modifies the president's. Decisions of Congress are subject to the pressures of different constituencies, so there is often much public squabbling over the designation of a Wilderness area.

Congress may also consider legislation for new Wilderness areas without first receiving agency or presidential recommendation. A member of Congress can introduce legislation that is his or her own or promoted by an interest group. Most recent designations have originated with interest groups.

While the designation of Wilderness is often a lengthy and complicated political process, the Wilderness Act accomplished an important task in shifting much of the responsibility for recommending and creating Wilderness from the agencies to the American people and the legislative process.[115] There is one school of thought in the Wilderness community that suggests that each new piece of legislation that designates Wilderness amends the 1964 Act. Since the act's passage, however, Congress has been hesitant to amend its core language, and thus its principles have survived with minimal alteration.

During the past decade, Congress made a number of significant additions to the NWPS. In 1993, nineteen areas in Colorado expanded the system by 750,000 acres. In 1994, President Clinton signed the California Desert Protection Act, adding 7.58 million acres. Additions in 2000 in Virginia, Colorado, Nevada, and Oregon increased the size of the NWPS by more than 1 million acres. In 2002, more than 500,000 acres in California, Colorado, Nevada, and South Dakota joined the system.[116] In 2004, a bill in Nevada added 768,000 acres.

History of Federal Wilderness Preservation

The frontier spirit drove American culture in the 1800s. "Go west, young man!" was the cry of the century as thousands of Americans headed west, first into the wilds of Kentucky, Ohio, Missouri, and other areas of the East, and later bridging the gap between the Mississippi River and the California coast. Appreciation for the inherent value of wild areas started slowly in America. Settlers were too busy carving their homes out of what was considered early on to be dark and dangerous wilderness.

It was not until after World War II, when Americans fell in love with the automobile and learned of the joys of recreation in primitive natural areas, that wilderness appreciation entered the mainstream. Until then, only a few individuals had a vision and held a passion for wilderness. These few had a profound influence on the development of Wilderness in the late nineteenth and early twentieth centuries. To the American public, the names of John Muir, Aldo Leopold, and Bob Marshall resonate as Wilderness heroes, but lesser-known advocates such as Arthur Carhart and Howard Zahniser were equally significant in the movement to create a system of protected Wilderness.

One of the first to lead passionate debate about preserving wilderness was John Muir, who founded the Sierra Club in 1892. To Muir, wilderness represented freedom, and in its remote beauty, it contained tremendous solace and solitude.

Voices for wilderness began to be heard from the ranks of the federal government. The Forest Service produced a lineage of men who pushed to protect areas administratively and later to obtain congressional consent for their designation. In 1919, Arthur Carhart, a Forest Service landscape architect, was assigned to draft a devel-

*Lyndon Johnson signed the Wilderness Act into law in 1964, extending new
protections to federally designated Wilderness Areas.*

opment plan for national forest land at Trappers Lake in
Colorado. After studying the area, Carhart reported that
the best use would be not to develop it at all. The agency
agreed and the area was protected. Carhart remained piv-
otal in early efforts to develop the NWPS.

A Forest Service forester named Aldo Leopold had
ideas similar to Carhart's. Leopold spent many years
attempting to create reservations for wilderness protection and primitive recreation in the West. In 1924,
Leopold's efforts led the Forest Service to establish the
first agency-protected roadless tract, 574,000 acres in the
Gila National Forest that were protected from road building and development. In 1929, the agency developed
guidelines for the management of these primitive areas

through the creation of the L-20 regulations, which established compatible and prohibited uses. These regulations represented the first time that any agency had attempted to turn wilderness management into something other than simply setting land aside.

Ten years later, the U regulations, proposed by Bob Marshall, tightened the purpose of Forest Service primitive areas. These regulations defined three classifications of national forest land—wilderness areas, wild areas, and roadless areas—and added timber development and mechanized access to the list of prohibited uses in primitive areas.

In the 1940s and 1950s, pressure built to create statutory protection for primitive areas. Marshall, Leopold, and a handful of eastern conservationists had established the Wilderness Society in 1935. This organization, led by Howard Zahniser in the 1950s and '60s, championed the cause for congressional legislation that would create a system to protect wilderness. Over the course of many years, Zahniser rallied the support of other conservation groups, such as the Sierra Club and National Wildlife Federation, and elected officials, such as Sen. Hubert Humphrey (D-MN) and Sen. Frank Church (D-ID). After eight years of vigorous debate and sixty-six drafts of the bill, the act passed Congress and was signed into law on September 3, 1964. Sadly, Zahniser died just four months before the Wilderness Act became the law of the land.

Wilderness Management

In the early days of implementing the Wilderness Act, many land managers and members of the public believed that the legislation mandated a hands-off approach to land management. In recent years, however, managers have recognized that there are significant threats to the

Howard Zahniser headed the Wilderness Society in the '50s and '60s and lobbied tirelessly on behalf of the Wilderness Act.

natural characteristics of Wilderness and to its "enduring" nature that must be managed. Some argue that global overpopulation is the number-one threat to Wilderness. Many managers worry about the impacts of increasing recreation in and around Wilderness. Threats originating outside of Wilderness pose problems as well, including acid rain, development of water resources, the introduction of exotic plant and animal species, and encroaching urbanization. Many in the agencies see the need for more direct management, although the object of management tends to be the external threats and uses, rather than the Wilderness itself.

The federal agencies struggle with a number of critical issues in attempting to meet the requirements of the Wilderness Act. A persistent lack of funding and inadequate staff resources hamper agency management. Many managers still believe that natural wildlands need no active management. Also lacking across the agencies is a solid baseline inventory of Wilderness areas, their status, and what they need in the way of management to maintain the characteristics that led them to designation. Without this information, the agencies are hard-pressed to determine, in a quantifiable way, whether the conditions of Wilderness are degrading, improving, or staying the same. They have no data on which to base and, importantly, defend management actions.

Wilderness management activities include the following:

- Providing public education, for example, Leave No Trace training, on Wilderness values and methods to minimize user impacts.
- Favoring Wilderness-dependent activities in management decisions.

- Generally not allowing permanent structures or installations, such as developed campgrounds, buildings, or radio antennae.
- Managing visitor use to protect the Wilderness resource. For example, agencies may provide trails to focus visitor travel in a certain area or place limits on group size or camping activity.
- Prohibiting the use of motorized vehicles and any form of mechanized transport unless they are determined to be the minimum requirement for the administration of the area, including cases of emergency.
- Excluding timber harvest.
- Allowing fires to burn under prescribed conditions, including both naturally occurring fires and those ignited by Wilderness managers.
- Taking measures to control fire, insects, and disease, when appropriate.
- Collecting information about resources in a manner compatible with the preservation of the Wilderness.

Other uses are allowed in Wilderness and must be managed:

- Hunting, fishing, and trapping under state and federal laws.
- Outfitting and guiding services under special use permits.
- Adequate access to private and state lands within Wilderness (referred to as in-holdings).
- Individual entry permits in heavily used Wilderness areas.
- Aircraft or motorboat use where it existed prior to Wilderness designation.

- Developing valid and existing mineral rights established prior to Wilderness designation.
- Livestock grazing where it existed prior to Wilderness designation.

Forest Service Wilderness. Of the four agencies, the Forest Service has the most highly developed and visible Wilderness program. The agency has also shown a long-standing commitment to Wilderness training and research, having spearheaded the creation of the Arthur Carhart National Wilderness Training Center and Aldo Leopold Research Institute, two organizations that are dedicated to the improvement of Wilderness management.[117] The Forest Service employs more people dedicated to Wilderness management than the other agencies and, along with the BLM, has a discrete budget line item for this purpose. Mandated by the National Forest Management Act, the Forest Service conducts new reviews during the forest-planning process in an effort to identify land that is suitable for Wilderness designation.

The year 2004 marked the fortieth anniversary of the Wilderness Act. As part of its acknowledgment of the important milestone, and in recognition of the poor state of many of its Wilderness areas, Forest Service chief Dale Bosworth initiated the Ten-Year Wilderness Challenge, a program to set goals and standards that will guide the agency to improve Wilderness stewardship measurably by the act's fiftieth anniversary.

National Park Service Wilderness. Wilderness is at the core of major ecosystems within national parks. Historically, however, the NPS has struggled with how to manage Wilderness within the context of existing national park law and regulation. To address this struggle, the agency established a Wilderness Task Force in 1993, charged with developing recommendations for improving stewardship within the agency. As a result, the NPS created an internal National Wilderness Steering Committee and an interagency Wilderness Policy Council. Both of these initiatives have helped establish more sensible, comprehensive policies to guide Wilderness management within the agency. Like the Forest Service, the NPS is a participant in the Carhart National Wilderness Training Center. Training and resources still need improvement, however. Half of all park system lands are designated Wilderness, but only one person is dedicated full-time to management of these lands, and the agency still must fulfill its legislative obligations related to review and recommendation.[118] Currently, 5.5 million acres of NPS land have been evaluated for Wilderness designation, but many have not yet been recommended by the agency to Congress, or have been recommended but not yet acted upon by Congress.[119]

BLM Wilderness. In 1976, Congress enacted the Federal Land Policy and Management Act, the first comprehensive organic law governing the BLM. Section 603 of the FLPMA directed the BLM to identify and inventory all public lands having Wilderness characteristics and values, as defined in the act, and study them for possible inclusion in the NWPS. As a result, in 1978, Congress designated the first BLM Wilderness areas: the Rogue River in Oregon and Santa Lucia in California. The first statewide BLM bill was enacted in Arizona in 1990, designating more than 1 million acres of BLM Wilderness.[120] With the creation of the National Landscape Conservation System in 2000, the agency signaled its intent to give greater management attention to special areas, including monuments and some citizen-proposed Wilderness lands.

Like many other aspects of public lands, Wilderness management in the BLM has unfortunately been subject to the significant forces of political will. The 1980 passage of the Alaska National Interest Lands Conservation Act left discretion to conduct Wilderness reviews in the state up to the secretary of the interior. In 1981, then Secretary James Watt, not known for his support for Wilderness, directed the BLM *not* to evaluate lands in Alaska. Secretary Bruce Babbitt lifted this order in 2001, and then Gale Norton reimposed it in 2003. Under FLPMA and NEPA, the BLM is still required to review Wilderness.[121]

In April 2003, the Interior Department settled a lawsuit brought by the state of Utah prohibiting the BLM from designating additional Wilderness Study Areas (WSAs), land considered suitable for designation that will be managed as such until Congress determines the outcome. This agreement effectively prevents the agency from determining whether millions of potentially suitable acres of western land will be protected by adding them to the NWPS. Conservation organizations went to court in 2004 to overturn this agreement.

As of 2004, the BLM manages 17.2 million acres as WSAs, and 6.5 million of the BLM's total 262 million acres benefit from the protection of Wilderness designation.

Fish and Wildlife Service Wilderness. The FWS completed its legally mandated Wilderness evaluation in 1974. The NWPS now includes 20.7 million refuge acres in sixty-six refuges. Another 5.4 million acres in thirty-two refuges have been recommended, but Congress has not yet acted. Conservation organizations, such as the Wilderness Society, believe that numerous refuge acres are suitable for Wilderness designation, but they have yet to be recommended. Although the refuge system was designed to protect wildlife and its habitat, significant acreage within the system has been under intense pressure for oil and gas development, mining, logging, and farming. These competing forces make Wilderness designation a significant challenge.

Wilderness in the FWS received a boost from the National Wildlife Refuge System Improvement Act, which requires the agency to prepare a comprehensive conservation plan for each refuge, including an evaluation of the potential for new Wilderness. The Interior Department stated, however, that it would attempt to exempt refuges in Alaska from this policy, increasing the pressure on such incredible areas as the Arctic National Wildlife Refuge.[122]

THE NATIONAL WILD AND SCENIC RIVERS SYSTEM

In 1968, Congress passed the Wild and Scenic Rivers Act, creating the National Wild and Scenic Rivers System (NWSRS) to preserve selected free-flowing rivers for the benefit and enjoyment of present and future generations.[123] This system was meant to add balance to the national policy of the time, which emphasized the construction of dams and other structures on many of the nation's rivers.

The act established three classes of river protection, based on the characteristics of the river at the time of designation:

> Wild rivers are free from impoundments (dams, diversions, etc.) and are generally inaccessible except by trail, where the watersheds are primitive and the shorelines are essentially undeveloped.
>
> Scenic rivers are free from impoundments in generally undeveloped areas, but are accessible in places by roads.

NOLS

The Wild and Scenic Rivers Act gave new protections to certain bodies of moving water in the United States.

Recreational rivers are readily accessible by road, with some shoreline development, and may have undergone some impoundment or diversion in the past.[124]

Rivers enter the system through either congressional designation or state nomination to the secretary of the interior, who also has the authority to designate protective status. Generally speaking, certain segments of rivers are nominated, rather than entire river corridors at one time. Congress initially designated 789 miles on eight rivers, and then began expanding the system, making substantial additions in the 1970s. ANILCA more than doubled the NWSRS through the designation of Alaska rivers in 1980. The system now includes 163 river units with 11,303 miles in thirty-eight states and Puerto Rico.

Management of the NWSRS emphasizes the protection of esthetic, scenic, historic, archaeological, and scientific values of the designated rivers—the values that led to their designation. Other uses of the river corridors within the system, such as hunting, fishing, or even mineral extraction, are permitted if they are consistent with the goals of the designation.

Initial NWSRS designations occurred mostly on rivers flowing through federal land. This simplified the designation process. One of the practical challenges of more recent designation is that rivers pass through many different areas of land, often owned and managed by different agencies, jurisdictions, or private parties. Upstream actions affect the rivers' downstream characteristics. Federal agencies have limited authority to purchase or otherwise obtain ownership of state or private lands that may fall within a wild and scenic designation. They are, however, directed to cooperate with state and local governments in the preparation of river management plans.

Mileage of Rivers Classified as Wild, Scenic, and Recreational, by State and Territory

State	Wild	Scenic	Recreational	Total
Alabama	36.40	25.00	0.00	61.40
Alaska	2,955.00	227.00	28.00	3,210.00
Arizona	18.50	22.00	0.00	40.50
Arkansas	21.50	147.70	40.80	210.00
California	685.80	199.60	986.85	1,872.25
Colorado	30.00	0.00	46.00	76.00
Connecticut	0.00	0.00	14.00	14.00
Delaware[a]	0.00	15.60	79.00	94.60
Florida	32.65	7.85	8.60	49.10
Georgia[a]	39.80	2.50	14.60	56.90
Idaho[a]	321.90	34.40	217.70	574.00
Illinois	0.00	17.10	0.00	17.10
Kentucky	9.10	0.00	10.30	19.40
Louisiana	0.00	19.00	0.00	19.00
Maine	92.50	0.00	0.00	92.50
Massachusetts	0.00	33.80	38.50	72.30
Michigan	79.00	277.90	267.90	624.80
Minnesota[a]	0.00	193.00	59.00	252.00
Mississippi	0.00	21.00	0.00	21.00
Missouri	0.00	44.40	0.00	44.40
Montana	161.90	66.70	139.40	368.00
Nebraska[a]	0.00	76.00	126.00	202.00
New Hampshire	0.00	13.50	24.50	38.00
New Jersey[a]	0.00	119.90	146.80	266.70
New Mexico	90.75	20.10	10.00	120.85
New York[a]	0.00	25.10	50.30	75.40
North Carolina[a]	44.40	95.50	52.00	191.90
Ohio	0.00	136.90	76.00	212.90
Oregon	635.65	381.40	798.05	1,815.10
Pennsylvania[a]	0.00	111.00	298.80	409.80
South Carolina[a]	39.80	2.50	14.60	56.90
South Dakota[a]	0.00	0.00	98.00	98.00
Tennessee	44.25	0.00	0.95	45.20
Texas	95.20	96.00	0.00	191.20
Washington	0.00	108.00	68.50	176.50
West Virginia	0.00	10.00	0.00	10.00
Wisconsin[a]	0.00	217.00	59.00	276.00
Wyoming	20.50	0.00	0.00	20.50
Puerto Rico	2.10	4.90	1.90	8.90
U.S. Total[b]	**5,350.60**	**2,457.20**	**3,495.10**	**11,302.90**

[a] This state shares mileage with some bordering states, where designated river segments are also state boundaries. Figures for each state reflect the total shared mileage, resulting in duplicate counting.

[b] Figure totals represent the actual totals of classified mileage in the United States and do not reflect duplicate counting of mileage of rivers running between state borders. Because the figures for individual states do reflect the shared mileage, the sum of the figures in each column exceeds the indicated column total.

Source: Vincent et al., *CRS Report for Congress.*

This process can be challenging, as different groups and individuals often have different goals and objectives for the same stretch of river or shoreline. For example, many western rivers flow through grazing allotments, providing a water source for livestock. Boaters who travel the waterways for recreation are often dismayed at the impacts they attribute to the livestock. It is the agency's responsibility to assess and manage impacts and balance such potentially competing uses. As with Wilderness designation, the nomination of rivers for the NWSRS is inherently a political process in which different groups and individuals strive to achieve their goals by influencing their representatives in Congress.

THE NATIONAL SCENIC TRAILS SYSTEM

The year 1968 was a busy one on Capitol Hill. In addition to passing the National Wild and Scenic Rivers Act, Congress also passed the National Trails System Act, which established the Appalachian and Pacific Crest National Scenic Trails and created the National Trails System (NTS) to provide outdoor recreation opportunities and promote the preservation of access to the nation's outdoor and historic resources. Similar to the NWSRS, the NTS includes classes of trails:

> National Scenic Trails provide outdoor recreation opportunities and preserve significant scenic, historic, natural, or cultural qualities.
>
> National Historic Trails follow travel routes of national historic significance (e.g., the Mormon Pioneer Trail, and the Lewis and Clark Trail).
>
> National Recreation Trails are accessible to urban areas on federal, state, or private lands.
>
> Connecting or Side Trails provide access to or between the other classes of trails.[125]

Passed the same year as the Wild and Scenic Rivers Act, the National Trails System Act gave birth to the Appalachian and Pacific Crest National Scenic Trails as well as a national network of smaller wilderness trails.

During the settlement of the West, trails served a functional purpose as routes for commerce and migration. Since the mid-1900s, when outdoor recreation became a popular national pastime, people have traveled trails to gain access to scenic terrain and immerse themselves in the great outdoors. In 1921, the first interstate trail, now the Appalachian National Scenic Trail, was introduced. In 1945, legislation to establish a national network of trails as part of a highway bill failed to gain enough momentum to make it to Congress. In 1958, in response to increasing population and the popularity of outdoor recreation, Congress created the Outdoor Recreation Resources Review Commission (ORRRC) to evaluate national recreation needs.[126] The commission learned that 90 percent of the nation's citizens participated in some form of outdoor recreation, and that walking for pleasure was the second most popular activity. As a result, President Lyndon Johnson initiated a quest in 1965 to "copy the Appalachian Trail in all parts of our country, and make full use of rights-of-way and other public paths."[127] The National Trails System Act soon followed.

Currently, the NTS consists of eight scenic trails and fifteen historic trails covering 40,000 miles, eight hundred recreational trails, and two connecting and side trails. The Park Service manages sixteen of the trails, including overall administration of the National Recreation Trails Program. The Forest Service manages four trails, the BLM one, and the NPS and BLM jointly administer two national historic trails. Responsibilities for managing these trails differ, depending on the class of trail.

Unlike the Wild and Scenic Rivers Act, the National Trails Act provides the secretaries of agriculture and the interior with the authority to acquire land through cooperative agreements or donations to help grow the NTS.

The act does not, however, authorize the purchase of land or provide sustained funding for the system. These factors have stymied the development of the NTS, preventing its growth and impeding operations on and maintenance of existing trails. Funding in recent years from the Federal Surface Transportation Program has helped, but the NTS program still suffers from a lack of authorized appropriations and the fact that the majority of the American public is unaware that the system exists. Trail supporters advocate for a nationwide promotion campaign to provide the public with information about the outstanding trail resources available to them. Others fear that such a campaign will lead to overuse of the system, taxing the already understaffed and underfunded program.

12

Land Management Challenges

The knowledge of the history behind federal lands and the experience of living with them help us evaluate the challenges and opportunities of the present and future. The mandates of the agencies are still largely the same as when set in statute decades ago. So, too, do many of the major issues of the past remain, including conflict over federal versus local control of public land, disagreement over how to implement agency missions, lack of funding for land management, and the need to manage competing demands. The demographic, social, and political dynamics of our country have changed dramatically, however. These changes have profoundly increased the challenge of managing public land "for the greater good." Even the task of defining that term has become a monumental challenge. Each of us has a different definition of "the greater good," and as citizen owners of public land, we each have the right to advocate for our unique definition. Though the issues surrounding federal lands are many, a few are at the forefront regarding the major public-land systems in the early twenty-first century and most need attention.

FEDERAL VERSUS LOCAL CONTROL

The tension between federal and local governments concerning the management of public land stretches back to the early 1900s, when Congress directed the land management agencies to stop disposing of federal land into state and private hands and manage the remainder for the benefit of all Americans. This shift left many western states hosting a great deal of federal land. Wyoming, for example, is 50 percent federal land, and Nevada is a whopping 92 percent.[128] As a result, much of the activity in these states—timber production, mineral development, recreation, hunting—occurs on federal land and as such is subject to the laws that govern this land. This leaves local leaders feeling that they have little control over what happens on much of the land around them. Since many of these states are rural, their economies are at least partially based on revenue generated from the development and use of natural resources. When local governments believe that federal laws affecting the management of the land around them interfere with their goals and vision, conflict arises.

Numerous struggles have occurred throughout the western states. In 1995, when the Fish and Wildlife Service reintroduced the gray wolf to Yellowstone National Park, ranchers, sportsmen, local governments, and many others in the surrounding areas fought bitterly, fearing the impact a healthy population of wolves would have on their livelihoods, lifestyles, and local economies. Ten years later, the wolf has made a remarkable recovery, and the FWS is prepared to remove it from the endangered species list on the condition that the states that are home to the wolf—Idaho, Montana, and Wyoming—submit management plans that meet the agency's requirements for a sustainable population. Asserting its independence, Wyoming submitted a plan in 2004 that the FWS would not approve and, rather than reach a compromise, filed suit against the FWS. The two sides remain stuck in a legal deadlock while the gray wolf remains on the endangered species list.

A similar situation played out in Minnesota, where the state and federal government argued over the implementation of a state management plan. Although Minnesota now has roughly 2,500 wolves, exceeding the recovery goal, the management situation remains in limbo.

EXTERNAL THREATS TO PUBLIC LANDS

The industrial revolution in this country gave birth to remarkable changes. The efficiency and productivity of the agriculture sector increased by leaps and bounds. New technology fueled an unprecedented wave in manufacturing, completely restructuring the nation's economy. Advances in medicine improved the lifespan of our population. Automobiles, for better or worse, became the glue that holds modern society together. Along with these accomplishments came significant growth in population. In 1960, the nation's population was 160 million. In 2004, that number swelled to 295 million.[129] This growth fueled subsequent increases in home construction, industrial development, and overall levels of domestic consumption that were never imagined a hundred years ago.

In the post–World War II years, the public lands supported this development. Sixty years later, these same lands stand to suffer from it. Population growth has led to a loss of open space as communities expand the edges of urban areas, encroaching on public land. At the same time, more people participate in a broader variety of activities on public land, leaving the agencies struggling

The significant growth in the use of public lands has strengthened support for wilderness areas even as it threatens their sustainability.

to keep pace with the number of visitors and the latest in recreation technology, and leaving the land exposed to impacts from unmanaged recreation. The production of increasing amounts of energy needed to sustain this growth has led to its own impacts: The signs of acid rain in alpine lakes and air quality impairment in national parks, forests, and wilderness areas are ever more visible.

Perhaps one of the most subtle but consequential threats to public land is the fact that most Americans are relatively unaware of their state and the important role they play in providing clear air and water, and fostering physical health and well-being. Some are even unaware that public lands exist—that a fundamental birthright of all Americans is ownership of land held in common for all of us. It is the American public, more than any other force, that has the capacity to affect how Congress and the federal agencies will manage these lands in the future. The public can determine whether or not our leaders in government will chart a course for long-term ecological sustainability of the national parks, forests, refuges, and public lands. To do so, they need to appreciate the importance of public land and understand the threats it faces.

GROWTH IN OUTDOOR RECREATION

All four federal land management agencies have witnessed a steady and significant increase in the demand for outdoor recreation on public land for the past several decades, and it is commonly said that we are "loving our public lands to death." Though more people participating in more outdoor recreation more often is a good thing for their overall health and well-being, managing the impact of increasing amounts of recreation has become a significant task for the agencies.

Managing Recreation Impacts

Each of the agencies manages recreation based on a set of internal guidelines or regulations, some of them specified by statute. The regulations determine overall management requirements designed to protect both the safety of visitors and the natural qualities of the environment.

A mechanism often used by the agencies to control use and thereby control or minimize impact is the commercial permit system, which determines how many people may visit public land under the guidance of a permitted operator, how long they may stay, where they may travel, and what they may do there. In some areas of the country where recreation use is particularly high, agencies set limits on the number of permits awarded to commercial operators. In other areas, they limit the allocation of use, restricting the number of days that an operator may bring visitors to a certain forest, refuge, or park. In still others, visitation is essentially unlimited.

As the popularity of outdoor recreation grows, and new technology such as cell phones and electronic mapping systems make recreationists feel more comfortable in the backcountry, agencies are tending toward more restrictive regulation. There is also a growing trend toward awarding commercial permits through a competitive process, a concept that causes great concern for smaller operators that cannot afford to compete with larger or more profitable companies. Of perhaps greater concern with this approach is the worry that agencies will place higher emphasis on the financial outcome of a permit than on the quality of performance of permit holders and their overall attention to protecting the natural resource on which their business depends.

While these management methods are sensible in many ways, they are fraught with conflict. Many commercial operators ask why they are targeted for restrictions when the general public is allowed to visit at their will, essentially unmanaged. Even some nonprofit or educational institutions are able to guide people in the outdoors without permits. The irony, permitted operators say, is that people who visit public lands with a permitted operator are less of a liability to the agencies. Permitted education-based operators, such as the National Outdoor Leadership School (NOLS), Outward Bound, and many university programs, emphasize teaching visitors about the public lands they visit and how to minimize their impacts through adherence to Leave No Trace principles and techniques.

Recreation has recently become the target of some organizations that believe that public lands cannot sustain the levels of use now common. This sets the stage for challenging conflict based on disagreement over some fundamental questions. What impacts does recreation cause? What can the land sustain? There is no universal agreement on the answers to such questions. It is incumbent on all users, including the general public and organized commercial service providers, to evaluate their own impacts and behave in appropriate ways that minimize them.

Public lands need the support of the constituencies formed by those who are passionate about recreation. Interest groups and individuals who value public lands for recreation build support for their funding and participate in public planning processes that help chart a course for future management. But there is a delicate point of balance—often a moving target—between providing access that meets the demand for recreation and managing recreation in a way that ensures the protection of the resource. The agencies are challenged on a daily basis to find and maintain this balance.

BALANCING COMPETING USES: THE MULTIPLE-USE CONUNDRUM

From the standpoint of providing "the greatest good of the greatest number," the concept of multiple-use management makes sense. Different groups and individuals have different needs and values, yet all have a right as citizens to enjoy and benefit from public lands. The Forest Service and the BLM, in particular, are charged with considering all possible uses of public lands in defining management goals. But as the population grows and the demands on public land diversify and intensify, meeting the needs of the public becomes ever more challenging. Add to this picture the influence of politics on management decisions, and fulfilling the multiple-use mission

FORESTRYIMAGES.ORG/JEFFERY J. WITCOSKY, USDA FOREST SERVICE

Nowhere is the tension between economic and recreational use of the wilderness more apparent than in logging operations on public land.

becomes quite daunting. How can an agency meet the needs of every member of the public, particularly when some uses are mutually exclusive?

Many of the traditional use conflicts have existed for decades. Managers of Yellowstone National Park have struggled for years to balance the needs of wildlife in winter with those of visitors who travel on snow machines, skis, and snowshoes. Elsewhere, boaters and river runners frequently object to the impacts they say result from the use of waterways by livestock. These types of conflicts are commonplace on public land and characterize the multiple-use conundrum. The agencies, caught in the middle of these conflicts, must answer a difficult question as objectively as possible: What types of use under what circumstances are appropriate on public land?

Some of the more challenging conflicts arise when traditional uses, such as grazing and mining, come into conflict with newer recreation-based uses. These traditional uses have a long history and, particularly in the West, are often tied to the provision of critical resources, local jobs, and economic growth. In spite of the growth in recreation and the contribution that recreation-related spending makes to federal and local economies, traditional industries still hold sway in the rural West, where many of the public land conflicts play out, and in Washington, where many of the decisions affecting public land are finalized. It is considerably easier, for example, to quantify the contributions of the oil and gas industry to the cash flow of Colorado or Montana than those of the recreation and tourism sector. Adding to the imbalance are the history and tradition that drive many western states' economies. Ranching and mineral development are mainstays in many western states, and people whose livelihoods have relied on these industries for many decades have trouble seeing recreation as a credible source of economic productivity. Without quantified proof of their contributions, the recreation industry has difficulty establishing its value compared with traditional uses of public land. And there is the added problem that recreation is fun. How can anything fun be taken seriously as an authentic component of a state's source of revenue, particularly in the West, where a physical work ethic has long been associated with economic value and success?

Organizations such as the Outdoor Industry Association (OIA) have formed in the past decade or two to represent members of the outdoor recreation industry who have an interest in the outcome of public land management decisions. The OIA is building a credible voice for recreation, highlighting the benefits to Americans of staying healthy in the outdoors, the increasing economic contributions of recreation, and its inherent sustainability compared with traditional extraction-oriented uses of the land.

Compounding the multiple-use conundrum are other often-debated questions: Where does preservation fit into the equation? Can it be considered a use? Are the values of biological diversity and ecological health ends in and of themselves? These philosophical and ethical questions stretch all the way back to the roots of the Forest Service, when Gifford Pinchot and John Muir first brought their differing viewpoints on forest management into the public realm.

The agencies attempt to handle these challenges through an open planning process that invites all members of the public to voice their needs and concerns. But though such a process provides a critical avenue for public input, and statutory and regulatory requirements provide some decision-making structure, in the end, the agencies are still faced with making difficult choices in an attempt to balance use. Whether they do so successfully is always the subject of great public debate and consternation. In trying to please everyone, the agencies often end up in the unenviable position of pleasing no one.

LACK OF APPROPRIATED FUNDING

Each fiscal year, Congress approves a budget to fund the U.S. government. The Departments of Agriculture and the Interior each receive a sum, portions of which are devoted to various management aspects of the Forest Service, NPS, FWS, and BLM. Appropriations shift depending on the goals and objectives of the White House and the elected officials who hold ranking positions on congressional committees overseeing the management of public land and appropriations.

Congressional appropriations for federal lands have largely stayed flat or declined in recent years, particularly for recreation management. According to the Forest Service, appropriations are no longer adequate to fund the agency fully. Congress currently provides $400 million annually to run the agency's recreation and heritage programs, for example, yet the total cost of the programs is $1.4 billion.[130] The administration's 2006 budget request for the Land and Water Conservation Fund, a program that provides federal funding for state recreation resources, decreased by $100 million from 2005 and falls far short of the administration's promise.

Land managers at the field level frequently point to these shortfalls when they are unable to take necessary management action, such as to improve visitor facilities or maintain backcountry trail systems. Staff resources in the Forest Service Wilderness Management Program are inadequate to cover the management needs of a system of 35 million acres. Local districts are at times unable to accept offers of volunteer projects, because the offices lack the staff power to manage the projects. Adding to the challenge, budgets are frequently cut in midyear, forcing staff reductions at critical times and putting the agencies in a very tough position. Though Congress and the administration are usually driving these cuts, it is the agencies that generally take the heat from the public for any reduction in service.

In an attempt to address these shortfalls, many groups have come forward over the years with ideas for alternative sources of funding public lands. In 1996, legislators passed a law that authorized the agencies to experiment with a recreation fee program that collected money from visitors to help fund on-the-ground projects. At the end of 2004, Congress modified this law and authorized it for ten years. Seen by many groups and individuals as an unfair additional tax on visitors to public lands, which they believe should be fully funded by congressional appropriations, the law was not well received by many members of the public and some western legislators.

Other groups propose that public lands should be funded by private-sector investment. They believe that by farming out the development and maintenance of facilities on public land, the public will be better served. Opponents believe that this approach amounts to placing the public domain at the mercy of private interests and fails to ensure the protection of the long-term health and sustainability of the natural resource. While opinions and ideas vary, one thing is certain: The significant budget deficit facing the country in the early twenty-first century ensures that the debates over public-land funding will continue for many years.

THE ROLES OF POLITICS AND SCIENCE IN DECISION MAKING

Public lands, even those managed for multiple use, have a hard time being all things to all people. This challenge has intensified as the number of people has increased and the variety and scope of the demands they place on public lands have expanded. Statutes and regulations provide a significant backbone when agencies must make difficult decisions that favor one use over another. Unfortunately, though, these tools cannot always provide the agencies with a clear answer to a conflict that involves diverse opinions.

It is natural, then, that agencies would turn to science in making management decisions, using quantifiable facts to support their choices. Several of the landmark land management statutes require the use of science in decision making. NEPA mandates the use of the best available science in performing environmental assessments and analyzing management options, but it does not clarify how an agency should interpret the science, or even define what is "best available."

This leaves the door open to interpretation. Conflict over what uses on public land are appropriate leads each side of an issue to interpret the science in a way that best fits its point of view. Even when the use of fact-based science makes the answer to a challenging question clear, the result may not be the politically desirable answer, and the objectives of political appointees begin to hold sway over the outcome.

In recent years, this pattern has led to an increasing number of disagreements heading to court to settle the conflict. For example, the National Park Service and the George W. Bush administration have been mired for years in a stalemate over the use of snow machines in Yellowstone and Grand Teton National Parks. Numerous scientific analyses have shown the likely negative impact from snow machine use on wildlife, air quality, and employee health in the park. Yet Interior Department officials have ordered the agency to complete additional studies aiming to support their stance that managed use will not harm the natural values of the park, and that the public has a right to travel by snow machine. Despite its expressed commitment to a preservation policy, the NPS has made modifications over time for political rather than ecological reasons.

A 2004 survey of scientists employed by the FWS uncovered some alarming statistics: More than 200 scientists said that they had been directed, at some point in their careers, to alter official findings to lessen protection for wildlife. In the Rocky Mountain region of the country, 83 percent of respondents to the survey said that they knew of cases in which political appointees of the Department of the Interior had "injected themselves" into agency scientific decisions.[131]

This kind of news is troubling, as the American public relies on the integrity of the land management agencies to sustain healthy public lands for the future. To some, this inherent fusing of politics and science is the result of a faulty policy structure. Erik Molvar of Biodiversity Conservation Alliance summarizes the issue succinctly: "You have agencies with professionals that are overseen by politicians that are beholden to special interests. This is what happens."[132]

WILDERNESS DESIGNATION AND MANAGEMENT

More than half of all designated Wilderness acres are within a day's drive of the nation's major cities. This is great news for the vast majority of people who enjoy outdoor recreation or simply love to be reminded that wild places exist. But proximity to large populations puts additional stress on Wilderness, compounding the management challenge. The Wilderness area of Mount Baker/Snoqualmie National Forest outside of Seattle supports upward of 720,000 visitors each year, more than any other Wilderness area in the national forest system.

According to statistics from the National Forest Foundation in 2004, recreational use in designated Wilderness increased tenfold in the past forty years, and more than 12 million people visit each year. More people want more access to these lands, but at the same time, increasing extraction of resources such as timber, oil, gas, and minerals from public land that is not protected is decreasing the total number of acres of wildlands suitable for primitive backcountry recreation, thus intensifying Wilderness visitation. All these factors increase the management load of the agencies, which have difficulty keeping up with the most basic operational needs, such as trail and campground maintenance.

Perhaps one of the most subtle but potentially harmful threats to Wilderness is the public's lack of awareness of it. According to a 2001 poll by Forest Service scientist Ken Cordell, only about half of all American adults know that the NWPS exists.[133] The National Forest Foundation tells us that the majority of Americans are unaware of the critical ecological, economic, and social benefits of Wilderness. Yet it is public support for protecting, maintaining, and expanding the NWPS that will keep it alive and healthy.

In 2004, America celebrated the fortieth anniversary of the Wilderness Act. At a national conference commemorating the event, two Forest Service representatives shared their views on what the nation must accomplish to ensure a healthy system of Wilderness in forty more years: First, we must be mindful of the need to practice restraint when it comes to managing and visiting Wilderness. The Wilderness Act, after all, mandates that Wilderness is an area of undeveloped federal land retaining its primeval character. Second, we must not waver from the legislative mandate set forth in the Wilderness Act to guide our management actions. Third, we must provide more structured and consistent professional training for federal Wilderness stewards. Fourth, we must develop a long-term monitoring system so that we know what we have accomplished and how far we need to go to protect

Wilderness. Finally, we must increase public awareness of the NWPS and its importance in preserving the future.[134] We have an obligation to introduce people to a public-land ethic and underscore the importance of intention when it comes to visiting Wilderness and wild places. We must connect people to the land in meaningful ways.

Designating New Wilderness

The National Wilderness Preservation System was first established with the designation of large swaths of national park and national forest land. High alpine ecosystems, arctic tundra, and the rock and ice above tree line in mountain states were obvious candidates. It was reasonably easy for people to agree that much of this remote and relatively pristine land was suitable for designation.

Representatives of Wilderness organizations, such as the Wilderness Society, say that our existing system of close to 106 million acres barely taps into the body of land that is suitable for protection. They believe that the NWPS will continue to grow, and that there are more than 100 million acres in Alaska and tens of millions within BLM land in the West that qualify for designation but have not yet been reviewed by the agencies or acted on by Congress.[135] Optimistic Wilderness proponents believe that over the next forty years, we will designate a significant number of new acres, mostly BLM land, perhaps doubling the size of the existing NWPS.

More recent designation efforts and the Wilderness negotiations of the future are likely to be more challenging, however. Many of the remote areas of the country that remain relatively wild and free from human disturbance have already been designated. The land at the center of recent Wilderness negotiations has tended to be

lower-elevation mountains and river valleys—land usually under great demand by a wide variety of users,
including ranchers, conservationists, boaters, motorized
vehicle enthusiasts, and mountain bikers. The result has
been negotiation, leading to what many consider compromise bills, or bills in which negotiators "give something to
get something."

There are widely ranging views on the prudence of
this approach to designating new lands, even within the
Wilderness community. Pragmatists believe that this is
the only way to set aside more Wilderness in today's
complicated, self-centered society. They define land eligi-
ble for designation more broadly. They realize that it is
not an ideal approach but move forward on the basis that
some additional Wilderness is better than none. Purists,
on the other hand, are dismayed by compromise bills.
Their belief is that Wilderness has a very specific character and serves a much higher purpose than any negoti-
ated use. They maintain that the most revered, pristine
wild places are not ours to bargain over, only to protect.

A few facets of new Wilderness designation are indis-
putable. First, Wilderness needs more legislative champions who will lead the charge on Capitol Hill. Second, a
great deal more education is necessary to raise the American public's awareness of the NWPS and its importance
to the nation's future. This is especially true as the population grows and demographics shift. A change in cultural
background of Americans will likely bring with it a different perception of Wilderness. Those who grew up in cultures without formally protected Wilderness may not
understand it or feel compelled to support it. Whereas
much of the Wilderness in the system today was the
result of a process driven by the agencies, future designation will require more initiative on the part of the public

and the conservation community. Informed American citizens who lobby their elected representatives for additional Wilderness will create the champions necessary to take new bills to the floors of Congress.

13

Land Management Opportunities

Wilderness management is 80 to 90 percent education and information and ten percent regulation.
—Former Forest Service chief Max Peterson

WILDERNESS EDUCATION

There is no disputing that educating visitors is an important part of the mission of each of the agencies charged with managing wilderness. Most agency leaders understand the value of educating people who visit public land.

Even so, the work of the federal agencies is grounded in statutory requirements, and to meet them, the agencies tend to rely heavily on regulation to ensure that they meet their management objectives. Education often seems to be more of an afterthought, a "nice-to-have" approach to managing land and minimizing impact, depending on how much money is available in the budget.

Why is this? There are some fairly simple reasons why agencies rely on regulation. In a broad sense, regulations provide land managers with the teeth necessary to enforce specified behavior, whereas education is a more

USDA FOREST SERVICE

Forest Rangers and other federal employees are responsible for educating the public about the wilderness and federal management policies.

passive approach to encourage people to do what they should. And people may or may not choose to comply with the suggestions of an education program. Also, education can be expensive, particularly as the population that engages in recreation and the activities they participate in become ever more diverse. Resource-strapped agencies are faced with producing large quantities of information in many media and multiple languages. Finally, the results of education programs can be difficult to measure, whereas regulatory measures such as tracking the number of citations awarded to correct behavior are simpler.

Regulation has its place. In some cases, as when setting boundaries on a designated Wilderness area, it may be the best way to manage behavior to ensure protection of the resource. Nevertheless, though having access to the "stick" when you need it is important, the education "carrot" is an extremely powerful tool because of its ability to affect behavior in positive, long-term ways.

In the case of backcountry recreation, education is a much more powerful tool than regulation in minimizing impact. Research indicates that backcountry behavior is the most important variable in determining visitors' ecological and social impact. Group-size limits established by land managers, a regulatory mechanism, do not by themselves translate to greater resource protection, as not all user groups adhere to minimum-impact principles equally. The paper "Wilderness Party Size Regulations," by a group of research scientists, stresses that not all groups create the same impact. Christopher Monz et al. say, "We are convinced that a large group of conscientious, experienced people, even with horses, can cause little impact, even less than a small group of people who are unconcerned or unknowledgeable."[136] Thus the techniques a group uses and how its members behave in the backcountry—factors influenced by education—are more important in determining impact than the size of the group, as established by regulation.

Since many of the impacts to public land can be traced directly to people's behavior, it makes sense that mitigating them ought to involve education. Though regulation plays an important role, it is critical to engage people in a learning process that will affect their behavior in a positive way far into the future.

The Role of Education Organizations
Outside of the context of a visitor center, agencies are limited in their ability to teach visitors proper backcountry

behavior. As a result, they tend to try to manage impact by regulating where visitors may travel, how many may travel there, and what they may do while they are there. Though these controls have merit, they do not, by themselves, send a strong educational message. In general, agencies lack the resources, in terms of both money and staff capability, to implement comprehensive education programs.

Outdoor education organizations and nonprofit institutions can play a critical role in filling this gap. The Sierra Club Outings Program, National Outdoor Leadership School, Outward Bound, Student Conservation Association, Yellowstone Association Institute, university programs, and many other organizations, through partnerships with the agencies, help them fulfill their education mandate.

Organizations such as these introduce people to the natural world, help them connect with it in meaningful and lasting ways, and instill in them a sense of responsibility to help sustain public lands. Many of them go a step further, introducing people to current issues affecting the land and teaching them how they can play a role in protecting it.

A prime example of this agency-nonprofit education partnership is the Leave No Trace Center for Outdoor Ethics (LNT). Originally founded in 1990 as a partnership program between the Forest Service and NOLS, LNT created a curriculum with core principles that minimize visitors' physical and social impact on the natural character of the outdoors. Having established a strong message based on this set of core behaviors, the center, formed as a separate nonprofit organization, now seeks to bring this message to the masses, raising the awareness of all visitors to public land, much in the way that Smokey the Bear became the symbol for preventing forest fire.

The Wilderness Act of 1964 identifies education as a fundamental purpose of Wilderness. Educational organizations help fulfill this purpose by teaching people how to take care of public land, how to appreciate it without harming it, and how to protect it for the future. In so doing, they promote the values of Wilderness and help raise the nation's collective awareness of the importance of the National Wilderness Preservation System.

Educational organizations must be careful to practice what they preach. It is easy to become caught in the altruistic nature of education and wildland protection. And it is easy to conclude that it is others' impact, and not their own, that degrades the resource they seek to protect. Experiential programs offered by outdoor educators are based on taking people into the backcountry to learn about it, appreciate it, and practice the skills necessary to protect it. In so doing, these programs must be quick to evaluate their own impact and slow to assume that because they are educating, they are immune to necessary restriction.

CITIZEN INVOLVEMENT

Given the extent of governmental control over public lands, the many layers of complex statutory and regulatory requirements that set the stage for decision making, and the often political nature of decisions, it is easy to be cynical about an individual's ability to effect change on public land. These lands are indeed public, however, and it is critical that the federal agencies hear from individuals and groups who have diverse opinions about how they should be managed. If most remain silent, the future of public lands will be determined by the interests of the few who most likely have a vested economic interest in the outcome of agency decisions. Americans in the conservation movement have been at the forefront, exercising their right and responsibility to participate actively in preserving our natural heritage. There are several concrete steps individuals can take to participate in public land management.

Explore and Learn

Explore wilderness and educate yourself. Get to know the area you are interested in firsthand. Hiking, backpacking, rafting, skiing, hunting, bird-watching, and other activities help you build an invaluable base of personal knowledge that allows you to speak, write, and represent an area with accuracy and confidence. Often people who spend time in an area know it better than the land managers who determine its future.

Knowing an area firsthand is not a prerequisite for participating in its management, however. You can appreciate an area without ever visiting it. Because federal lands belong to all citizens, not just local residents or users, everyone can be a vicarious explorer through reading and learning about an area. You should not feel hindered from acting as a steward for any place that has touched you in any way.

Stay Informed

Once you have identified specific wildlands that you care about, take steps to stay informed about the condition of and plans for the area. Significant issues, such as proposals to drill for oil and gas in the Arctic National Wildlife Refuge, command national media attention. Popular magazines and newspapers often carry stories about these issues. If your concern is more local or regional in scope, or you don't live in the vicinity of the area, identify the organizations that monitor the places and issues that interest you, and become a member. Read their newsletters and visit their websites. They keep a close eye on the status of land management activities and routinely inform members about concerns or threats to an area, as well as opportunities to participate in a public-comment process.

Some organizations have a regional focus. The Greater Yellowstone Coalition focuses on roughly 10 million acres in three western states, two national parks, and six national forests that surround and include Yellowstone and Grand Teton National Parks. The Southern Utah Wilderness Alliance (SUWA) tracks issues and organizes citizen involvement in the canyon country of Utah. Other groups target issues affecting an entire state, such as the Wyoming Outdoor Council and the Alaska Center for the Environment. These groups often send out newsletters and action alerts.

Check out the websites of national groups, such as the Sierra Club, Wilderness Society, and National Wildlife Federation. Many host local chapters or have regional offices that can provide you with more specific information about an area.

Placing your name on land management agency mailing lists is another useful way to keep abreast of current issues. You can usually specify the types of activities you are interested in, such as Wilderness management, timber sales, or oil and gas development. Once an agency has your name, it should let you know when it will hold public-comment periods on proposed activities.

Take Action

Taking action can be as simple as writing a letter to an agency or the editor of your local paper, or as challenging as organizing a grassroots campaign, becoming an outdoor educator, or going to work for a land management agency. Regardless of the scope, taking action can be effective and rewarding, and it is a legitimate exercise of your citizenship.

There are many avenues for effective public input. A personal visit with a land manager or legislator responsible for, or having influence on, a decision is the most direct way, but this requires advance planning and often some travel. The best and quickest way to start taking action is to write a letter to a public official. Though some advocates may disagree, letters are effective, particularly when they are written by individuals expressing specific concerns about a specific place, speaking from personal experience. The following guidelines are helpful for writing effective letters:

- Convey your main point clearly in the first sentence or two. Don't make the reader wade through a lengthy letter to uncover your principal concern.
- Organize your points to be concise and specific about the issue. Refer to the specific land management unit by name, and cite the specific management action or legislation that concerns you.
- Refer to your personal experience with the issue or area. Mention specific landforms, such as rivers, lakes, and mountains, to add credibility to your position.
- Be polite and professional. Use the correct salutation; for example, elected officials should be addressed as "The Honorable Senator John Jones." Take the time to confirm the correct title and spelling of the name of your recipient.
- Include your return address on the letter. Legislators are likely to write you a letter in return.

- Write letters not only when you want to ask for something or offer constructive criticism, but also to express support for a proposed action or position the official has taken.

Taking action can also mean volunteering your time for the organizations working on the issues that concern you. This can take the form of preparing informational mailings, working to increase membership, or organizing a major lobbying effort in Washington, D.C.

No matter what the level of your motivation or how much time you have available, you will be able to find a comfortable level of involvement in public-land policy issues. If you exercise the privilege to explore and enjoy the nation's wildlands, exercise your responsibility as a citizen to protect and conserve the wilderness that is your heritage as well.

APPENDIX A

Where to Go for Additional Information

The following is a sampling of the many websites that provide access to mountains of information about public lands:

Wilderness.net, a national clearinghouse of information about Wilderness *www.wilderness.net*
USDA Forest Service *www.fs.fed.us*
National Park Service *www.nps.gov*
Bureau of Land Management *www.blm.gov*
U.S. Fish and Wildlife Service *www.fws.gov*
U.S. Department of the Interior *www.doi.gov*
Elected officials on Capitol Hill *www.congress.org*
National Parks Conservation Association *www.npca.org*
National Wildlife Federation *www.nationalwildlife.org*
Sierra Club *www.sierraclub.org*
The Wilderness Society *www.tws.org* (also see the exhaustive list of environmental organizations at *www.wilderness.org/links/list.htm#research*)
Ecology Hall of Fame *www.ecotopia.org*
Izaak Walton League of America *www.iwla.org*
International Journal of Wilderness *http://ijw.wilderness.net*

WILD Foundation *www.wild.org*
Natural Resources Defense Council *www.nrdc.org*
Library of Congress: The Evolution of the Conservation
  Movement
  http://lcweb2.loc.gov/ammem/amrvhtml/conshome.html
Leave No Trace Center for Outdoor Ethics *www.lnt.org*
National Outdoor Leadership School *www.nols.edu*
University of Idaho: Wilderness Archives
  www.lib.uidaho.edu/specialcollections/Wilderness.Archives.
  html
World Conservation Union *www.iucn.org*
United Nations Educational, Scientific and Cultural
  Organization (UNESCO): World Network of Bios-
  phere Reserves *www.unesco.org/mab/wnbr.htm*
United Nations Environment Programme *www.unep.org*
Aldo Leopold Wilderness Research Institute
  http://leopold.wilderness.net
USDA Forest Service: Rocky Mountain Research Station
  www.fs.fed.us/rm
Arthur Carhart National Wilderness Training Center
  http://carhart.wilderness.net
Center for Environmental Philosophy *www.cep.unt.edu*
International Association for Environmental Philosophy
  www.environmentalphilosophy.org
International Society for Environmental Ethics
  www.cep.unt.edu/ISEE.html
High Country News *www.hcn.org*
Forest Service Employees for Environmental Ethics
  www.fseee.org

APPENDIX B

Public Involvement in the National Environmental Policy Act Process

In 1969, Congress passed the National Environmental Policy Act (NEPA), which provides the legal basis for public involvement in land management agency decisions. NEPA directs the agencies to determine the environmental effects of proposed actions, commonly through either an environmental impact statement (EIS) or environmental assessment (EA). The primary purpose of an EIS, as stated in federal regulation, is as follows:

> to serve as an action-forcing device to insure that the policies and goals defined in [NEPA] are infused into the ongoing programs and actions of the Federal Government. It shall provide full and fair discussion of significant environmental impacts and shall inform decision makers and the public of the reasonable alternatives which would avoid or minimize adverse impacts or enhance the quality of the human environment.[137]

EISs are used for assessing proposals that may have significant impacts on the environment. An agency may determine at the outset that an EIS is not necessary, in which case it will prepare an EA. The EA explains why a project will not have a significant environmental impact, and a finding of no significant impact (FONSI) will be prepared and released to the public.

The standard NEPA process involves six steps:

1. Notice of intent. The managing agency publishes a notice of intent in the public Federal Register. This identifies the agency's intent to prepare an EIS.
2. Solicitation of scoping comments. The agency determines the scope of issues it will address in the EIS and the associated issues. It invites the public and other government agencies to provide comments during this phase.
3. Draft EIS. The agency prepares a draft EIS, which contains analysis of the proposed action, offers alternative approaches, defines resources that may be affected by each alternative, projects environmental consequences, and addresses issues raised during scoping. Law requires the agency to provide and analyze at least three alternatives. The heart of the EIS is the analysis of alternatives.
4. Public-comment period. The agency must release the draft EIS and provide the public with ninety days to submit comments on the alternatives.
5. Final EIS. After evaluating the comments on the draft EIS, the agency carries out any additional analysis needed to address them and prepares a final EIS.
6. Record of decision. The final EIS is accompanied by a record of decision, which clearly states the agency's final intent with regard to the proposed project or plan.

Appendix C

The Wilderness Act

Public Law 88-577
88th Congress, S. 4
September 3, 1964

AN ACT

To establish a National Wilderness Preservation System for the permanent good of the whole people, and for other purposes.

Be it enacted by the Senate and House of Representatives of the United States of America in Congress assembled,

SHORT TITLE
Section 1. This Act may be cited as the "Wilderness Act."

WILDERNESS SYSTEM ESTABLISHED
STATEMENT OF POLICY
Sec. 2. (a) In order to assure that an increasing population, accompanied by expanding settlement and growing mechanization, does not occupy and modify all areas within the United States and its possessions, leaving no lands designated for preservation and protection in their natural condition, it is hereby declared to be the policy of

the Congress to secure for the American people of present and future generations the benefits of an enduring resource of wilderness. For this purpose there is hereby established a National Wilderness Preservation System to be composed of federally owned areas designated by Congress as "wilderness areas", and these shall be administered for the use and enjoyment of the American people in such manner as will leave them unimpaired for future use as wilderness, and so as to provide for the protection of these areas, the preservation of their wilderness character, and for the gathering and dissemination of information regarding their use and enjoyment as wilderness; and no Federal lands shall be designated as "wilderness areas" except as provided for in this Act or by a subsequent Act.

(b) The inclusion of an area in the National Wilderness Preservation System notwithstanding, the area shall continue to be managed by the Department and agency having jurisdiction thereover immediately before its inclusion in the National Wilderness Preservation System unless otherwise provided by Act of Congress. No appropriation shall be available for the payment of expenses or salaries for the administration of the National Wilderness Preservation System as a separate unit nor shall any appropriations be available for additional personnel stated as being required solely for the purpose of managing or administering areas solely because they are included within the National Wilderness Preservation System.

DEFINITION OF WILDERNESS

(c) A wilderness, in contrast with those areas where man and his own works dominate the landscape, is hereby recognized as an area where the earth and its community of life are untrammeled by man, where man himself is a visitor who does not remain. An area of wilderness is further defined to mean in this Act an area of undeveloped Federal land retaining its primeval character and influence, without permanent improvements or human habitation, which is protected and managed so as to preserve its natural conditions and which (1) generally appears to have been affected primarily by the forces of nature, with the imprint of man's work substantially unnoticeable; (2) has outstanding opportunities for solitude or a primitive and unconfined type of recreation; (3) has at least five thousand acres of land or is of sufficient size as to make practicable its preservation and use in an unimpaired condition; and (4) may also contain ecological, geological, or other features of scientific, educational, scenic, or historical value.

NATIONAL WILDERNESS PRESERVATION SYSTEM—EXTENT OF SYSTEM

Sec. 3. (a) All areas within the national forests classified at least 30 days before the effective date of this Act by the Secretary of Agriculture or the Chief of the Forest Service as "wilderness," "wild," or "canoe" are hereby designated as wilderness areas. The Secretary of Agriculture shall—

(1) Within one year after the effective date of this Act, file a map and legal description of each wilderness area with the Interior and Insular Affairs Committees of the United States Senate and the House of Representatives, and such descriptions shall have the same force and effect as if included in this Act: Provided, however, That correction of clerical and typographical errors in such legal descriptions and maps may be made.

(2) Maintain, available to the public, records pertaining to said wilderness areas, including maps and legal

descriptions, copies of regulations governing them, copies of public notices of, and reports submitted to Congress regarding pending additions, eliminations, or modifications. Maps, legal descriptions, and regulations pertaining to wilderness areas within their respective jurisdictions also shall be available to the public in the offices of regional foresters, national forest supervisors, and forest rangers.

(b) The Secretary of Agriculture shall, within ten years after the enactment of this Act, review, as to its suitability or nonsuitability for preservation as wilderness, each area in the national forests classified on the effective date of this Act by the Secretary of Agriculture or the Chief of the Forest Service as "primitive" and report his findings to the President. The President shall advise the United States Senate and House of Representatives of his recommendations with respect to the designation as "wilderness" or other reclassification of each area on which review has been completed, together with maps and a definition of boundaries. Such advice shall be given with respect to not less than one-third of all the areas now classified as "primitive" within three years after the enactment of this Act, not less than two-thirds within seven years after the enactment of this Act, and the remaining areas within ten years after the enactment of this Act. Each recommendation of the President for designation as "wilderness" shall become effective only if so provided by an Act of Congress. Areas classified as "primitive" on the effective date of this Act shall continue to be administered under the rules and regulations affecting such areas on the effective date of this Act until Congress has determined otherwise. Any such area may be increased in size by the President at the time he submits his recommendation to the Congress by not more than five thousand acres with no more than one thousand two hundred and eighty acres of such increase in any one compact unit; if it is proposed to increase the size of any such area by more than five thousand acres or by more than one thousand two hundred and eighty acres in any one compact unit the increase in size shall not become effective until acted upon by Congress. Nothing herein contained shall limit the President in proposing, as part of his recommendations to Congress, the alteration of existing boundaries of primitive areas or recommending the addition of any contiguous area of national forest lands predominantly of wilderness value. Not withstanding any other provisions of this Act, the Secretary of Agriculture may complete his review and delete such area as may be necessary, but not to exceed seven thousand acres, from the southern tip of the Gore Range–Eagles Nest Primitive Area, Colorado, if the Secretary determines that such action is in the public interest.

(c) Within ten years after the effective date of this Act the Secretary of the Interior shall review every roadless area of five thousand contiguous acres or more in the national parks, monuments and other units of the national park system and every such area of, and every roadless island within, the national wildlife refuges and game ranges, under his jurisdiction on the effective date of this Act and shall report to the President his recommendation as to the suitability or nonsuitability of each such area or island for preservation as wilderness. The President shall advise the President of the Senate and the Speaker of the House of Representatives of his recommendation with respect to the designation as wilderness of each such area or island on which review has been completed, together with a map thereof and a definition of its boundaries. Such advice shall be given with respect to not less than one-third of the areas and islands to be reviewed under this subsection within three years after enactment of this Act, not less than two-thirds within seven years of enactment of this Act, and the remainder within ten years of enactment of this Act. A recommendation of the President for designation as wilderness shall become effective only if so provided by an Act of Congress. Nothing contained herein shall, by implication or otherwise, be construed to lessen the present statutory authority of the Secretary of the Interior with respect to the maintenance of roadless areas within units of the national park system.

(d) (1) The Secretary of Agriculture and the Secretary of the Interior shall, prior to submitting any recommendations to the President with respect to the suitability of any area for preservation as wilderness—

(A) give such public notice of the proposed action as they deem appropriate, including publication in the Federal Register and in a newspaper having general circulation in the area or areas in the vicinity of the affected land;

(B) hold a public hearing or hearings at a location or locations convenient to the area affected. The hearings shall be announced through such means as the respective Secretaries involved deem appropriate, including notices in the Federal Register and in newspapers of general circulation in the area: Provided, That if the lands involved are located in more than one State, at least one hearing shall be held in each State in which a portion of the land lies;

(C) at least thirty days before the date of a hearing advise the Governor of each State and the governing board of each county, or in Alaska the borough, in which the lands are located, and Federal departments and agencies concerned, and invite such officials and Federal agencies to submit their views on the proposed action at the hearing or by not later than thirty days following the date of the hearing.

(2) Any views submitted to the appropriate Secretary under the provisions of (1) of this subsection with respect to any area shall be included with any recommendations to the President and to Congress with respect to such area.

(e) Any modification or adjustment of boundaries of any wilderness area shall be recommended by the appropriate Secretary after public notice of such proposal and public hearing or hearings as provided on subsection (d) of this section. The proposed modification or adjustment shall then be recommended with map and description thereof to the President. The President shall advise the United States Senate and the House of Representatives of his recommendations with respect to such modification or adjustment and such recommendations shall become effective only on the same manner as provided for in subsections (b) and (c) of this section.

USE OF WILDERNESS AREAS

Sec. 4. (a) The purposes of this Act are hereby declared to be within and supplemental to the purposes for which national forests and units of the national park and national wildlife refuge systems are established and administered and—

(1) Nothing in this Act shall be deemed to be in interference with the purpose for which national forests are established as set forth in the Act of June 4, 1897 (30 Stat. 11), and the Multiple Use Sustained-Yield Act of June 12, 1960 (74 Stat. 215).

(2) Nothing in this Act shall modify the restrictions and provisions of the Shipstead-Nolan Act (Public Law 539, Seventy-first Congress, July 10, 1930; 46 Stat. 1020),

the Thye-Blatnik Act (Public Law 733, Eightieth Congress, June 22, 1948; 62 Stat. 568), and the Humphrey-Thye-Blatnik-Andersen Act (Public Law 607, Eighty-fourth Congress, June 22, 1965; 70 Stat. 326), as applying to the Superior National Forest or the regulations of the Secretary of Agriculture.

(3) Nothing in this Act shall modify the statutory authority under which units of the national park system are created. Further, the designation of any area of any park, monument, or other unit of the national park system as a wilderness area pursuant to this Act shall in no manner lower the standards evolved for the use and preservation of such park, monument, or other unit of the national park system in accordance with the Act of August 25, 1916, the statutory authority under which the area was created, or any other Act of Congress which might pertain to or affect such area, including, but not limited to, the Act of June 8, 1906 (34 Stat. 225; 16 U.S.C. 432 et seq.); section 3(2) of the Federal Power Act (16 U.S.C. 796(2)); and the Act of August 21, 1935 (49 Stat. 666; 16 U.S.C. 461 et seq.).

(b) Except as otherwise provided in this Act, each agency administering any area designated as wilderness shall be responsible for preserving the wilderness character of the area and shall so administer such area for such other purposes for which it may have been established as also to preserve its wilderness character. Except as otherwise provided in this Act, wilderness areas shall be devoted to the public purposes of recreational, scenic, scientific, educational, conservation, and historical use.

PROHIBITION OF CERTAIN USES

(c) Except as specifically provided for in this Act, and subject to existing private rights, there shall be no commercial enterprise and no permanent road within any wilderness area designated by this Act and, except as necessary to meet minimum requirements for the administration of the area for the purpose of this Act (including measures required in emergencies involving the health and safety of persons within the area), there shall be no temporary road, no use of motor vehicles, motorized equipment or motorboats, no landing of aircraft, no other form of mechanical transport, and no structure or installation within any such area.

SPECIAL PROVISIONS
(d) The following special provisions are hereby made:

(1) Within wilderness areas designated by this Act the use of aircraft or motorboats, where these uses have already become established, may be permitted to continue subject to such restrictions as the Secretary of Agriculture deems desirable. In addition, such measures may be taken as may be necessary in the control of fire, insects, and diseases, subject to such conditions as the Secretary deems desirable.

(2) Nothing in this Act shall prevent within national forest wilderness areas any activity, including prospecting, for the purpose of gathering information about mineral or other resources, if such activity is carried on in a manner compatible with the preservation of the wilderness environment. Furthermore, in accordance with such program as the Secretary of the Interior shall develop and conduct in consultation with the Secretary of Agriculture, such areas shall be surveyed on a planned, recurring basis consistent with the concept of wilderness preservation by the Geological Survey and the Bureau of Mines to determine the mineral values, if any, that may be present; and the results of such surveys shall be

made available to the public and submitted to the President and Congress.

(3) Not withstanding any other provisions of this Act, until midnight December 31, 1983, the United States mining laws and all laws pertaining to mineral leasing shall, to the extent as applicable prior to the effective date of this Act, extend to those national forest lands designated by this Act as "wilderness areas"; subject, however, to such reasonable regulations governing ingress and egress as may be prescribed by the Secretary of Agriculture consistent with the use of the land for mineral location and development and exploration, drilling, and production, and use of land for transmission lines, waterlines, telephone lines, or facilities necessary in exploring, drilling, producing, mining, and processing operations, including where essential the use of mechanized ground or air equipment and restoration as near as practicable of the surface of the land disturbed in performing prospecting, location, and, in oil and gas leasing, discovery work, exploration, drilling, and production, as soon as they have served their purpose. Mining locations lying within the boundaries of said wilderness areas shall be held and used solely for mining or processing operations and uses reasonably incident thereto; and hereafter, subject to valid existing rights, all patents issued under the mining laws of the United States affecting national forest lands designated by this Act as wilderness areas shall convey title to the mineral deposits within the claim, together with the right to cut and use so much of the mature timber therefrom as may be needed in the extraction, removal, and beneficiation of the mineral deposits, if needed timber is not otherwise reasonably available, and if the timber is cut under sound principles of forest management as defined by the national forest rules and regulations, but

each such patent shall reserve to the United States all title in or to the surface of the lands and products thereof, and no use of the surface of the claim or the resources therefrom not reasonably required for carrying on mining or prospecting shall be allowed except as otherwise expressly provided in this Act: Provided, That, unless hereafter specifically authorized, no patent within wilderness areas designated by this Act shall issue after December 31, 1983, except for the valid claims existing on or before December 31, 1983. Mining claims located after the effective date of this Act within the boundaries of wilderness areas designated by this Act shall create no rights in excess of those rights which may be patented under the provisions of this subsection. Mineral leases, permits, and licenses covering lands within national forest wilderness areas designated by this Act shall contain such reasonable stipulations as may be prescribed by the Secretary of Agriculture for the protection of the wilderness character of the land consistent with the use of the land for the purposes for which they are leased, permitted, or licensed. Subject to valid rights then existing, effective January 1, 1984, the minerals in lands designated by this Act as wilderness areas are withdrawn from all forms of appropriation under the mining laws and from disposition under all laws pertaining to mineral leasing and all amendments thereto.

(4) Within wilderness areas in the national forests designated by this Act, (1) the President may, within a specific area and in accordance with such regulations as he may deem desirable, authorize prospecting for water resources, the establishment and maintenance of reservoirs, water-conservation works, power projects, transmission lines, and other facilities needed in the public interest, including the road construction and maintenance

essential to development and use thereof, upon his determination that such use or uses in the specific area will better serve the interests of the United States and the people thereof than will its denial; and (2) the grazing of livestock, where established prior to the effective date of this Act, shall be permitted to continue subject to such reasonable regulations as are deemed necessary by the Secretary of Agriculture.

(5) Other provisions of this Act to the contrary notwithstanding, the management of the Boundary Waters Canoe Area, formerly designated as the Superior, Little Indian Sioux, and Caribou Roadless Areas, in the Superior National Forest, Minnesota, shall be in accordance with the general purpose of maintaining, without unnecessary restrictions on other uses, including that of timber, the primitive character of the area, particularly in the vicinity of lakes, streams, and portages: Provided, That nothing in this Act shall preclude the continuance within the area of any already established use of motorboats.

(6) Commercial services may be performed within the wilderness areas designated by this Act to the extent necessary for activities which are proper for realizing the recreational or other wilderness purposes of the areas.

(7) Nothing in this Act shall constitute an express or implied claim or denial on the part of the Federal Government as to exemption from State water laws.

(8) Nothing in this Act shall be construed as affecting the jurisdiction or responsibilities of the several States with respect to wildlife and fish in the national forests.

STATE AND PRIVATE LANDS WITHIN WILDERNESS AREAS

Sec. 5. (a) In any case where State-owned or privately owned land is completely surrounded by national forest lands within areas designated by this Act as wilderness, such State or private owner shall be given such rights as may be necessary to assure adequate access to such State-owned or privately owned land by such State or private owner and their successors in interest, or the State-owned land or privately owned land shall be exchanged for federally owned land in the same State of approximately equal value under authorities available to the Secretary of Agriculture: Provided, however, That the United States shall not transfer to a state or private owner any mineral interests unless the State or private owner relinquishes or causes to be relinquished to the United States the mineral interest in the surrounded land.

(b) In any case where valid mining claims or other valid occupancies are wholly within a designated national forest wilderness area, the Secretary of Agriculture shall, by reasonable regulations consistent with the preservation of the area as wilderness, permit ingress and egress to such surrounded areas by means which have been or are being customarily enjoyed with respect to other such areas similarly situated.

(c) Subject to the appropriation of funds by Congress, the Secretary of Agriculture is authorized to acquire privately owned land within the perimeter of any area designated by this Act as wilderness if (1) the owner concurs in such acquisition or (2) the acquisition is specifically authorized by Congress.

GIFTS, BEQUESTS, AND CONTRIBUTIONS

Sec. 6. (a) The Secretary of Agriculture may accept gifts or bequests of land within wilderness areas designated by this Act for preservation as wilderness. The Secretary of Agriculture may also accept gifts or bequests of land adjacent to wilderness areas designated by this Act for preservation as wilderness if he has given sixty days advance notice thereof to the President of the Senate and the

Speaker of the House of Representatives. Land accepted by the Secretary of Agriculture under this section shall become part of the wilderness area involved. Regulations with regard to any such land may be in accordance with such agreements, consistent with the policy of this Act, as are made at the time of such gift, or such conditions, consistent with such policy, as may be included in, and accepted with, such bequest.

(b) The Secretary of Agriculture or the Secretary of the Interior is authorized to accept private contributions and gifts to be used to further the purpose of this Act.

ANNUAL REPORTS

Sec. 7. At the opening of each session of Congress, the Secretaries of Agriculture and Interior shall jointly report to the President for transmission to Congress on the status of the wilderness system, including a list and descriptions of the areas in the system, regulations in effect, and other pertinent information, together with any recommendations they may care to make.

Approved September 3, 1964.

APPENDIX D

Federal Land by State and Agency

State	Forest Service	National Park Service	Fish and Wildlife Service	Bureau of Land Mgmt.
Alabama	665,978	16,917	59,528	111,369
Alaska	21,980,905	51,106,274	76,774,229	85,953,625
Arizona	11,262,350	2,679,731	1,726,280	11,651,958
Arkansas	2,591,897	101,549	361,331	295,185
California	20,741,229	7,559,121	472,338	15,128,485
Colorado	14,486,977	653,137	84,649	8,373,504
Connecticut	24	6,775	872	0
Delaware	0	0	26,126	0
District of Columbia	0	6,949	0	0
Florida	1,152,913	2,482,441	977,997	26,899
Georgia	864,623	40,771	480,634	0
Hawaii	1	353,292	299,380	0
Idaho	20,465,345	761,448	92,165	11,846,931
Illinois	293,016	12	140,236	224
Indiana	200,240	11,009	64,613	0
Iowa	0	2,708	112,794	378
Kansas	108,175	731	58,695	0
Kentucky	809,449	94,169	9,078	0
Louisiana	604,505	14,541	545,452	321,734
Maine	53,040	76,273	61,381	0
Maryland	0	44,482	45,030	548
Massachusetts	0	33,891	16,797	0
Michigan	2,865,103	632,368	115,244	74,807
Minnesota	2,839,693	142,863	547,421	146,658
Mississippi	1,171,158	108,417	226,039	56,212
Missouri	1,487,307	63,436	70,859	2,094
Montana	16,923,153	1,221,485	1,328,473	7,964,623
Nebraska	352,252	5,909	178,331	6,354
Nevada	5,835,284	777,017	2,389,616	47,874,294
New Hampshire	731,942	15,399	15,822	0
New Jersey	0	38,505	71,197	0
New Mexico	9,417,693	379,042	385,052	13,362,538

table continued on page 214

State	Forest Service	National Park Service	Fish and Wildlife Service	Bureau of Land Mgmt.
New York	16,211	37,114	29,081	0
North Carolina	1,251,674	394,833	423,948	0
North Dakota	1,105,977	71,650	1,566,026	59,642
Ohio	236,360	20,552	8,875	0
Oklahoma	399,528	10,200	170,032	2,136
Oregon	15,665,881	197,301	572,590	16,125,145
Pennsylvania	513,399	51,239	10,048	0
Rhode Island	0	5	2,179	0
South Carolina	616,970	27,488	162,958	0
South Dakota	2,013,447	263,644	1,300,465	274,960
Tennessee	700,764	362,133	116,966	0
Texas	755,363	1,184, 046	534,319	11,833
Utah	8,180,405	2,099,083	112,027	22,867,896
Vermont	389,200	21,513	33,230	0
Virginia	1,662,124	336,950	132,989	805
Washington	9,273,381	1,933,972	344,956	402,355
West Virginia	1,033,882	62,707	18,595	0
Wisconsin	1,525,978	74,010	236,470	159,982
Wyoming	9,238,067	2,393,281	101,857	17,354,151
Territories	28,149	33,179	1,766,965	0
Total	**192,511,012**	**79,005,557**	**95,382,237**	**261,457,325**

Source: Vincent et al., *CRS Report for Congress.*

Federally Designated Wilderness Acreage by State and Agency

State	Total Acreage	Forest Service	National Park Service	Fish and Wildlife Service	Bureau of Land Mgmt.
Alabama	41,367	41,367	0	0	0
Alaska	57,522,408	5,753,448	33,079,611	18,689,349	0
Arizona	4,528,973	1,345,008	444,055	1,343,444	1,396,466
Arkansas	153,655	116,578	34,933	2,144	0
California	14,154,062	4,430,849	6,122,045	9,172	3,591,996
Colorado	3,345,091	3,142,035	60,466	3,066	139,524
Connecticut	0	0	0	0	0
Delaware	0	0	0	0	0
Florida	1,426,327	74,495	1,300,580	51,252	0
Georgia	485,484	114,537	8,840	362,107	0
Hawaii	155,590	0	155,590	0	0
Idaho	4,005,712	3,961,667	43,243	0	802
Illinois	32,782	28,732	0	4,050	0
Indiana	12,945	12,945	0	0	0
Iowa	0	0	0	0	0
Kansas	0	0	0	0	0
Kentucky	18,097	18,097	0	0	0
Louisiana	17,025	8,679	0	8,346	0
Maine	19,392	12,000	0	7,392	0
Maryland	0	0	0	0	0
Massachusetts	2,420	0	0	2,420	0
Michigan	249,219	91,891	132,018	25,310	0
Minnesota	815,952	809,772	0	6,180	0
Mississippi	6,046	6,046	0	0	0
Missouri	71,113	63,383	0	7,730	0
Montana	3,443,038	3,372,503	0	64,535	6,000
Nebraska	12,429	7,794	0	4,635	0
Nevada	1,581,871	823,585	0	0	758,286

table continued on page 216

State	Total Acreage	Forest Service	National Park Service	Fish and Wildlife Service	Bureau of Land Mgmt.
New Hampshire	102,932	102,932	0	0	0
New Jersey	10,341	0	0	10,341	0
New Mexico	1,625,117	1,388,262	56,392	39,908	140,555
New York	1,363	0	1,363	0	0
North Carolina	111,419	102,634	0	8,785	0
North Dakota	39,652	0	29,920	9,732	0
Ohio	77	0	0	77	0
Oklahoma	23,113	14,543	0	8,570	0
Oregon	2,274,152	2,086,504	0	925	186,723
Pennsylvania	9,031	9,031	0	0	0
Rhode Island	0	0	0	0	0
South Carolina	60,681	16,671	15,010	29,000	0
South Dakota	77,570	13,426	64,144	0	0
Tennessee	66,349	66,349	0	0	0
Texas	85,333	38,483	46,850	0	0
Utah	800,614	772,894	0	0	27,720
Vermont	59,421	59,421	0	0	0
Virginia	177,214	97,635	79,579	0	0
Washington	4,317,133	2,569,391	1,739,763	839	7,140
West Virginia	80,852	80,852	0	0	0
Wisconsin	42,323	42,294	0	29	0
Wyoming	3,111,232	3,111,232	0	0	0
Territories	0	0	0	0	0
Total	**105,176,917**	**34,807,965**	**43,414,402**	**20,699,338**	**6,255,212**

Source: Vincent et al., *CRS Report for Congress.*

Endnotes

1. Immanuel Kant, *Groundwork of the Metaphysics of Morals* (Cambridge: Cambridge University Press, 1998), xv.
2. Aldo Leopold, *A Sand County Almanac: with Essays on Conservation from Round River* (New York: Ballantine Books, 1977), 262.
3. Ibid.
4. Wilderness Act, Section 2(c).
5. Gary Snyder, "The Etiquette of Freedom," *Sierra* [Volume # 74] (September–October 1989): 76.
6. Bill Devall and George Sessions, *Deep Ecology: Living as if Nature Mattered* (Salt Lake City: Gibbs M. Smith, 1985), 65.
7. Aldo Leopold, *Round River* (New York: Oxford University Press, 1993), 145–46.
8. Wallace Stegner, letter to Outdoor Recreation Resources Review Commission in support of the Wilderness Act.
9. Edward Abbey, *The Journey Home* (New York: E. P. Dutton, 1977), 229.
10. Gen. 1:28.
11. Char Miller, *Gifford Pinchot and the Making of Modern Environmentalism* (Washington DC: Island Press, 2001), 338.

12. Roderick Nash, *Wilderness and the American Mind* (New Haven: Yale University Press, 1982), 161.
13. Lynn White Jr., "The Historical Roots of Our Ecological Crisis," *Science* 155 (March 10, 1967): 1203–07.
14. Wilderness Act, Section 1(a).
15. Thomas Berry, *The Dream of the Earth* (San Francisco: Sierra Club Books, 1988), 1.
16. www.archives.gov/publications/prologue/1985/spring/chief-seattle.html.
17. Chief Seattle of the Squamish Tribe, "In Search of Understanding" (Speech delivered to mark the transfer of ancestral Indian lands to the U.S. government, 1854).
18. Devall and Sessions, *Deep Ecology*, 104–5.
19. Stephen Fox, *John Muir and His Legacy* (Boston: Little, Brown, 1981), 52–53.
20. Leopold, *A Sand County Almanac, and Sketches Here and There* (New York: Oxford University Press, 1949), 210.
21. Roderick Nash, *The Rights of Nature: A History of Environmental Ethics* (Madison, WI: University of Wisconsin Press, 1989), 75.
22. John C. Hendee, George H. Stankey, and Robert C. Lucas, *Wilderness Management, Second Edition* (Golden, CO: North American Press, 1990), 108.
23. Mark Woods, "Federal Wilderness Preservation in the United States: The Preservation of Wilderness?" in *The Great New Wilderness Debate*, ed. J. Baird Callicott and Michael P. Nelson (Athens, GA: The University of Georgia Press, 1998), 137.
24. Arturo Gomez-Pompa and Andrea Kaus, "Taming the Wilderness Myth," in Callicott and Nelson, 297.
25. Wilderness Act, Section 2(c).

26. John Muir, *Our National Parks* (Boston and New York: Houghton, Mifflin, and Co., 1901), 285.

27. Dave Foreman, "Wilderness Areas for Real," in Callicott and Nelson, 404.

28. See, e.g., George Perkins Marsh, *Man and Nature; or, Physical Geography as Modified by Human Action* (1864; reprint, Cambridge, MA: Belknap Press of Harvard University, 1965); Nash, *Wilderness and the American Mind*; and White, "Historical Roots of Our Ecological Crisis."

29. Henry David Thoreau, *The Portable Thoreau*, rev. ed., ed. Carl Bode (Viking Penguin, 1947), 592, 609.

30. Henry David Thoreau, *The Maine Woods* (Boston: Ticknor and Fields, 1864), 20–21.

31. Ralph Waldo Emerson, "Nature," in *Nature: Addresses and Lectures* (Boston: J. Munroe, 1849).

32. Clyde Fisher, in *Natural History* 31, no. 5 (September–October 1931): 510.

33. John Burroughs, "Touches of Nature" in *Birds and Poets: with Other Papers* (New York: Hurd and Houghton, 1877), 49.

34. Muir, *Our National Parks*, 56.

35. John Muir, *My First Summer in the Sierra* (New York: Penguin Books, 1987), 157.

36. Muir, *Our National Parks*, 364–365.

37. Quoted in Peter Landres et al., *Monitoring Selected Conditions Related to Wilderness Character: A National Framework* (Fort Collins, CO: USDA Forest Service, Rocky Mountain Research Station, 2005), 17.

38. Bob Marshall. "The Problem of the Wilderness," *Scientific Monthly* 30, no. 2 (February 1930): 147.

39. Quoted in Governor's Commission on the Future of Florida's Environment, *Facing Florida's Environmental Future* (Tallahassee, FL: Governor's Com-

mission on the Future of Florida's Environment, 1990).

40. Arthur Carhart National Wilderness Training Center, carhart.wilderness.net/index.cfm?fuse=arthur Carhart.

41. Leopold, *A Sand County Almanac: with Essays on Conservation from Round River*, 239–40.

42. 16 U.S.C. Section 1.

43. Leopold, *A Sand County Almanac and Sketches Here and There*, 223–24.

44. Ibid., 200.

45. Roderick Nash, "Why Wilderness?" in *For the Conservation of the Earth: Proceedings of the Fourth World Wilderness Conference,* ed. Vance Martin (Golden, CO: Fulcrum Publishing, 1988), 199–200.

46. Nash, *Wilderness and the American Mind*, 261.

47. Sigurd F. Olson, *Sigurd F. Olson: The Meaning of Wilderness,* ed. David Backes (Minneapolis, MN: University of Minnesota Press, 2001), 40–41.

48. Leopold, *Sand County Almanac*, 202–3.

49. Joy A. Palmer, *Fifty Key Thinkers on the Environment* (New York: Routledge, 2001), 214.

50. Ibid.

51. Devall and Sessions, *Deep Ecology*, 65.

52. Rachel Carson, *The Sea around Us* (New York: Oxford University Press: 2003), xiii.

53. See Peter Singer, *Animal Liberation: A New Ethics for Our Treatment of Animals* (New York: New York Review, 1975).

54. See J. E. Lovelock, *Gaia: A New Look at Life on Earth* (New York: Oxford University Press, 1987).

55. Andrew Light and Holmes Rolston III, eds., *Environmental Ethics: An Anthology* (Malden, MA: Blackwell Publishers, Ltd., 2003), 176.

56. Val Plumwood, *Feminism and the Mastery of Nature* (New York: Routledge, 1994), 196.
57. Christopher D. Stone, *Should Trees Have Standing? Toward Legal Rights for Natural Objects* (Palo Alto, CA: Tioga Publishing Company, 1988), 9.
58. Ibid., 73–75.
59. Terry Tempest Williams, Statement before the Senate Subcommittee on Forest and Public Lands Management regarding the Utah Public Lands Management Act of 1995, Washington, DC, July 13, 1995.
60. Jack Turner, "In Wilderness Is the Preservation of the World," in Callicott and Nelson, 624–26.
61. Wilderness Act, Section 2(c).
62. Ken H. Cordell, Michael A. Tarrant, and Gary T. Green, "Is the Public Viewpoint of Wilderness Shifting?" *International Journal of Wilderness* 9, no. 2 (August 2003): 27–32.
63. John B. Loomis and Robert Richardson, "Economic Values of the U.S. Wilderness System: Research Evidence to Date and Questions for the Future," *International Journal of Wilderness* 7, no. 1 (April 2001): 31–34.
64. Michael Frome, "To Rekindle Love of the Beautiful in Public Policy and Professional Performance," *International Journal of Wilderness* 7, no. 2 (August 2001): 6.
65. Laura Waterman, "On Writing Wilderness Ethics: Some Further Musings of the 'Spirit of Wildness,'" *International Journal of Wilderness* 9, no. 2 (August 2003): 23.
66. www.lnt.org/about/index.html.
67. Kendall Clark and Susan Kozacek, "How Do Your Personal Wilderness Values Rate?" *International Journal of Wilderness* 3, no. 1 (March 1997): 12.

68. Leopold, *A Sand County Almanac: with Essays on Conservation from Round River*, 138–39.
69. Nash, *Rights of Nature*, 44.
70. John Gookin and Darran Wells, *NOLS Environmental Education Notebook* (Lander, WY: National Outdoor Leadership School, 2002), 13.
71. Joseph Wood Krutch, *The Desert Year* (Tucson, AZ: University of Arizona Press, 1951), 37.
72. Morgan Hite, "Briefing for Entry into a More Harsh Environment" (Unpublished essay, 1989).
73. E. F. Schumacher, *Small Is Beautiful: Economics as if People Mattered* (New York: Harper and Row, 1973), 33, 39.
74. Wendell Berry, *Home Economics* (Berkeley, CA: North Point Press, 1987), 139.
75. Carol Hardy Vincent, et al. *CRS Report for Congress* (Congressional Research Service, Library of Congress, 2004), Summary.
76. Ibid., 6.
77. Federal Land Policy and Management Act, Section 102(a).
78. Vincent et al., *CRS Report*, 2.
79. Ibid., 12.
80. www.fs.fed.us.aboutus/meetfs.shtml.
81. Multiple-Use Sustained Yield Act, PL 86–517, Section 1.
82. Tara Wilfong, "Management of National Forests," *Forest Service Centennial* (2005): 72–73.
83. USDA Forest Service Range Management, *Grazing Statistical Summary FY 2002* (January 2003).
84. Multiple-Use Sustained Yield Act, PL 86–517, Section 1.
85. Wilfong, "Management of National Forests," 64.
86. Vincent et al., *CRS Report*, 12.

87. U.S. Department of the Interior, "Department of the Interior Quick Facts" http://mits.doi.gov/quickfacts/tables_all.cfm.

88. National Park Service Organic Act, 39 stat. 535, U.S.C. Section 1.

89. Robert B. Keiter, "Preserving Nature in the National Parks: Law, Policy, and Science in a Dynamic Environment," *Denver University Law Review* 74, no. 3 (1997): 653.

90. Ibid., 666.

91. National Park Service, *Annual Wilderness Report 2002–2003* (National Wilderness Steering Committee, NPS, Department of the Interior, 2003), Appendix 1.

92. National Park Service, http://www.nps.gov.

93. Vincent et al., *CRS Report*, 12.

94. U.S. Department of the Interior, "Department of the Interior Quick Facts," http://mits.doi.gov/quick facts/tables_all.cfm.

95. Taylor Grazing Act, PL 73-482, Subchapter 1, Sections 315, 315a.

96. Federal Land Policy and Management Act, PL 86–517, Section 102.

97. Vincent et al., *CRS Report*, 31.

98. Ibid., 11.

199. Ibid., 34.

100. Ibid., 35.

101. Ibid.

102. Ibid., 12.

103. U.S. Department of the Interior, "U.S. Department of the Interior University," http://www.doiu.nbc.gov.

104. U.S. Department of the Interior, "Department of the Interior Quick Facts," http://mits.doi.gov/quick facts.

105. Ibid.
106. Vincent et al., *CRS Report*, 43.
107. National Wildlife Refuge System Improvement Act, Public Law 105–57, Section 4.
108. Ibid., Section 5.
109. Robert L. Fischman, "The National Wildlife Refuge System and the Hallmarks of Modern Organic Legislation," *Ecology Law Quarterly* 29, no. 3 (2002), 486.
110. Ibid., 34.
111. Ben Beach et al., eds., *The Wilderness Act Handbook, 40th anniv. ed.* (Washington, D.C.: Wilderness Society, 2004), 3.
112. Ibid.
113. Wilderness Act, PL 88–577, Section 2(a).
114. Ibid., Section 2(c).
115. Beach et al., *Wilderness Act Handbook*, 1.
116. Ibid., 15.
117. Ibid., 27.
118. Ibid., 36.
119. Ibid., 35.
120. Ibid., 13.
121. Ibid., 31.
122. Ibid., 39.
123. Wild and Scenic Rivers Act, P.L. 90–542.
124. Vincent et al., *CRS Report*, 64.
125. Ibid., 68.
126. Ibid.
127. Ibid.
128. Vincent et al., *CRS Report*, 3.
129. Ken Cordell et al., *Recreation Statistics Update* (Athens, GA: USDA Forest Service, 2004), 1.
130. Barbara Stahura, "Forest Service Recreation," *Forest Service Centennial* (2004):109.

131. Whitney Royster, "Survey: Scientists Told to Alter Findings," *Casper [Wyoming] Star-Tribune*, February 11, 2005.

132. Ibid.

133. Ken Cordell, "Wilderness in Contemporary America" (Eighth Annual Ecotourism in Alaska Conference, February 2001); www.srs.fs.fed.us/trends.

134. Rebecca Oreskes and Karen Woodsum (40th Anniversary National Wilderness Conference, Lake George, New York, October 10–13, 2004).

135. Beach et al., *Wilderness Act Handbook*, 1.

136. Christopher Monz et al., "Wilderness Party Size Regulations: Implications for Management and a Decisionmaking Framework," *USDA Forest Service Proceedings*, RMRS-P-15, vol. 4 (2000): 266.

137. Code of Federal Regulations, Title 40, Section 1502.1.

Bibliography

Abbey, Edward. 1977. *The Journey Home.* New York: E. P. Dutton.

American Recreation Coalition. 2004. *Roper Report.* The Recreation Roundtable.

Beach, Ben, Leslie Jones, Bart Koehler, and Jay Watson, eds. 2004. *The Wilderness Act Handbook: 40th Anniversary Edition.* Washington, DC: Wilderness Society.

Berry, Thomas. 1988. *The Dream of the Earth.* San Francisco: Sierra Club Books.

Berry, Wendell. 1987. *Home Economics.* Berkeley, CA: North Point Press.

Brown, David E., and Neil B. Carmony. 1990. *Aldo Leopold's Southwest.* Albuquerque: University of New Mexico Press.

Brown, Lester R., et al. 1990. *State of the World, 1990.* New York: W. W. Norton Company.

Burroughs, John. 1877. *Birds and Poets: with Other Papers* New York: Hurd and Houghton.

Callicott, J. Baird, and Michael P. Nelson, eds. 1998. *The Great New Wilderness Debate.* Athens: University of Georgia Press.

Carson, Rachel. 1951. *The Sea around Us.* New York: Oxford University Press.

————. 1962. *Silent Spring.* Boston: Houghton Mifflin.

Cheever, Federico. 1999. "Symposium: Wilderness Act of 1964: Reflections, Applications, and Predictions." *Denver University Law Review.*

————. 1997. "The United States Forest Service and National Park Service: Paradoxical Mandates, Powerful Founders, and the Rise and Fall of Agency Discretion." *Denver University Law Review.*

Clark, Kendall, and Susan Kozacek. 1997. "How Do Your Personal Wilderness Values Rate?" *International Journal of Wilderness* 3, no. 1 (March).

Coffin, James B. 2005. *Federal Parks and Recreation* 23, no. 4.

The Conservation Foundation. 1987. *State of the Environment: A View toward the Nineties. A Report from the Conservation Foundation.* Sponsored by the Charles Stewart Mott Foundation. Washington, DC.

Cordell, Ken. 2001. "Wilderness in Contemporary America." Eighth Annual Ecotourism in Alaska Conference.

Cordell, Ken, C. Betz, M. Fly, G. Green, B. Stephens. 2004. *Recreation Statistics Update.* USDA Forest Service, Southern Research Station, Athens, GA.

Cordell, Ken H., Michael A. Tarrant, and Gary T. Green. 2003. "Is the Public Viewpoint of Wilderness Shifting?" *International Journal of Wilderness* 9, no. 2 (August).

Dawson, Chad, Rebecca Oreskes, Mary Wagner, and Karen Woodsum. 40th Anniversary National Wilderness Conference, October 10–13, 2004, Lake George, New York.

Devall, Bill. 1988. *Simple in Means, Rich in Ends: Practicing Deep Ecology.* Salt Lake City: Gibbs-Smith Publisher.

Devall, Bill, and George Sessions. 1985. *Deep Ecology: Living as if Nature Mattered.* Salt Lake City: Gibbs M. Smith.

Emerson, Ralph Waldo. 1849. *Nature: Addresses and Lectures.*

Fischman, Robert L. 2002. "The National Wildlife Refuge System and the Hallmarks of Modern Organic Legislation." *Ecology Law Quarterly* 29, no. 3.

Fisher, Clyde. *Natural History* 31, no. 5 (September–October 1931).

Fox, Stephen. 1981. *John Muir and His Legacy.* Boston: Little, Brown.

Frome, Michael. 2001. "To Rekindle Love of the Beautiful in Public Policy and Professional Performance." *International Journal of Wilderness* 7, no. 2 (August).

Frome, Michael, Horace M. Albright, Dennis E. Teeguarden, and the Regents of the University of California, Berkeley. 1988. *Conservators of Hope: The Horace M. Albright Conservation Lectures.* Moscow: University of Idaho Press.

Geisel, Theodore Seuss. 1971. *The Lorax.* New York: Random House.

Glover, James M. 1986. *A Wilderness Original: The Life of Bob Marshall.* Seattle: The Mountaineers.

Gookin, John. 2003. *NOLS: Wilderness Educator Notebook.* Lander, WY: National Outdoor Leadership School.

Gookin, John, ed. 2003. *Wilderness Wisdom: Quotes for Inspirational Exploration.* National Outdoor Leadership School. Mechanicsburg, PA: Stackpole Books.

Gookin, John, and Darran Wells. 2002. *NOLS: Environmental Education Notebook.* Lander, WY: National Outdoor Leadership School.

Governor's Commission on the Future of Florida's Environment. 1990. *Facing Florida's Environmental Future.* Tallahassee, FL: Governor's Commission on the Future of Florida's Environment.

Hampton, Bruce, and David Cole. 2003. *Soft Paths.* Third Edition. Harrisburg, PA: Stackpole Books.

Harmon, David, ed. 1989. *Mirror of America: Literary Encounters with the National Parks.* Boulder, CO: Roberts Rinehart.

Harvey, Mark. 1999. *The National Outdoor Leadership School's Wilderness Guide.* New York, NY: Fireside.

Hendee, John C., George H. Stankey, and Robert C. Lucas. 1990. *Wilderness Management,* 2nd ed., rev. Golden, CO: North American Press.

Hite, Morgan. 1989. "Briefing for Entry into a More Harsh Environment." Unpublished essay.

Holmer, Steve. "A Conservation History of the National Forests." Unified Forest Defense Campaign.

Hungerford, H., and T. Volk. 1990. "Changing Learner Behavior through Environmental Education." *Journal of Environmental Education.*

Keiter, Robert B. 1997. "Preserving Nature in the National Parks: Law, Policy, and Science in a Dynamic Environment." *Denver University Law Review* 74, no. 3.

Krutch, Joseph Wood. 1951. *The Desert Year.* Tucson: University of Arizona Press.

Laitos, Jan G. 1997. "National Parks and the Recreation Resource." *Denver University Law Review* 74, no. 3.

Landres, Peter, Steve Boutcher, Linda Merigliano, Chris Barns, Denis Davis, Troy Hall, Steve Henry, Brad Hunter, Patrice Janiga, Mark Laker, Al McPherson, Douglas S. Powell, Mike Rowan, and Susan Sater. 2005. *Monitoring Selected Conditions Related to Wilderness Character: A National Framework.* Fort Collins, CO: USDA Forest Service, Rocky Mountain Research Station.

Leopold, Aldo. 1937. Conservationist in Mexico. *American Forests* (March).

Leopold, Aldo. 1977. *A Sand County Almanac: with Essays on Conservation from Round River.* New York: Ballantine Books.

————. 1949. *A Sand County Almanac, and Sketches Here and There.* New York: Oxford University Press.

————. 1993. *Round River.* New York: Oxford University Press.

Light, Andrew, and Holmes Rolston III, eds. 2003. *Environmental Ethics: An Anthology.* Malden, MA: Blackwell Publishers.

Loomis, John B., and Robert Richardson. 2001. "Economic Values of the U.S. Wilderness System: Research Evidence to Date and Questions for the Future." *International Journal of Wilderness* 7, no. 1 (April).

Lopez, Barry Holstun. 1979. *Desert Notes: Reflections in the Eye of a Raven.* Kansas City, MO: Andrews and McMeel.

Lorbiecki, Marybeth. 1996. *Aldo Leopold: A Fierce Green Fire.* Helena, MT: Falcon Publishing Company.

Lovelock, J. E. 1987. *Gaia: A New Look at Life on Earth.* Oxford, New York: Oxford University Press.

Marsh, George Perkins. 1864. *Man and Nature; or, Physical Geography as Modified by Human Action.* Cambridge, MA: Belknap Press of Harvard University. 1965.

Marshall, Bob. "The Problem of the Wilderness." *Scientific Monthly* 30, no. 2 (February 1930).

Martin, Vance, ed. 1988. *For the Conservation of the Earth: Proceedings of the Fourth World Wilderness Conference.* Golden, CO: Fulcrum Publishing.

Matsumoto, Sarah, Cara Pike, Tom Turner, and Ray Wan. 2003. *Citizens' Guide to the Endangered Species Act.* Washington, DC: Earthjustice.

Miller, Char. 2001. *Gifford Pinchot and the Making of Modern Environmentalism.* Washington, DC: Island Press.

Monz, Christopher, Richard Brame, David Cole, Joseph Roggenbuck, and Andrew Yoder. 2000. "Wilderness Party Size Regulations: Implications for Management and a Decisionmaking Framework." *USDA Forest Service Proceedings*, RMRS-P-15, vol. 4.

Muir, John. 1901. *Our National Parks*. Boston and New York: Houghton, Mifflin, and Co.

————. 1997. *My First Summer in the Sierra*. New York: Penguin Books.

Nash, Roderick. 1982. *Wilderness and the American Mind*. New Haven, CT: Yale University Press.

————. 1988. "Why Wilderness?" In *For the Conservation of the Earth,* edited by Vance Morton, Speech delivered at the Fourth World Wilderness Congress, Denver, CO, September 11–18, 1987.

————. 1989. *The Rights of Nature, A History of Environmental Ethics*. Madison, WI: University of Wisconsin Press.

National Outdoor Leadership School. 1985. *NOLS Conservation Practices*. Lander, WY: National Outdoor Leadership School.

National Park Service. 2002. "Visitor Use Summary." www.nps.org.

————. 2003. *Annual Wilderness Report 2002–2003*. National Wilderness Steering Committee, National Park Service, Department of the Interior.

Nelson, Richard. 1989. *The Island Within*. San Francisco: North Point Press.

Oelschlaeger, Max. 1991. *The Idea of Wilderness*. New Haven, CT: Yale University Press.

Olson, Sigurd F. 2001. *The Meaning of Wilderness: Essential Articles and Speeches*, ed. David Backes, Minneapolis: University of Minnesota Press.

Palmer, Joy A. 2001. *Fifty Key Thinkers on the Environment*. New York, NY: Routledge.

Plumwood, Val. 1994. *Feminism and the Mastery of Nature*. New York: Routledge.

Public Land Law Review Commission. 1970. *One Third of the Nation's Land*. Washington, DC: Public Land Law Review Commission.

Rolston, Holmes III. 1986. *Philosophy Gone Wild: Essays in Environmental Ethics*. Buffalo, NY: Prometheus Books.

———. 1988. *Environmental Ethics: Duties to and Values in the Natural World*. Philadelphia: Temple University Press.

Royster, Whitney. 2005. "Survey: Scientists Told to Alter Findings." *Casper [Wyoming] Star-Tribune*. February 11.

Sax, Joseph L. 1980. *Mountains without Handrails: Reflections on the National Parks*. Ann Arbor, MI: University of Michigan Press.

Schumacher, E. F. 1973. *Small Is Beautiful: Economics as if People Mattered*. New York: Harper and Row.

Seattle, Chief of the Squamish Tribe. 1854. "In Search of Understanding." Speech delivered to mark the transfer of ancestral Indian lands to the U.S. government.

Singer, Peter. 1975. *Animal Liberation: A New Ethics for our Treament of Animals*. New York: New York Review.

———. 1975. *Practical Ethics*. New York: Avon Books.

Smith, T. V., and Marjorie Grene, ed. 1940. *Berkeley, Hume, and Kant*. Chicago and London: University of Chicago Press.

Snyder, Gary. 1974. *Turtle Island*. New Directions Publishing Corp.

———. 1989. "The Etiquette of Freedom." *Sierra* (September–October).

Stahura, Barbara. 2004. "Forest Service Recreation." *Forest Service Centennial Magazine*.

Steen, Harold K. 2004. *The Chiefs Remember: The Forest Service, 1952–2001*. Durham, NC: Forest History Society.

Stegner, Wallace. Letter to (ORRRC) in support of Wilderness Act.

Stone, Christopher D. 1988. *Should Trees Have Standing? Toward Legal Rights for Natural Objects.* Palo Alto, CA: Tioga Publishing Company.

Thoreau, Henry David. 1947. *The Portable Thoreau,* rev. ed., ed. Carl Bode. Viking Penguin.

———. 1864. *The Maine Woods.*

Tilton, Buck. 2003. *The Leave No Trace Master Educator Handbook.* Lander, WY: National Outdoor Leadership School and the Leave No Trace Center for Outdoor Ethics.

U.S. Fish and Wildlife Service. 2001. *National Survey of Fishing, Hunting, and Wildlife-Associated Recreation.*

USDA Forest Service. 2004. *The Greatest Good.* A Forest Service Centennial Film. www.fs.fed.us/greatestgood.

———. 2002. "Management's Discussion and Analysis." www.fs.fed.us.

USDA Forest Service Range Management. January 2003. *Grazing Statistical Summary FY 2002.*

Van Matre, Steve, and Bill Weiler. 1983. *The Earth Speaks: An Acclimatization Journal.* Warrenville, IL: Institute for Earth Education.

Vincent, Carol Hardy, Pamela Baldwin, Kori Calvert, M. Lynne Corn, Ross W. Gorte, Sandra L. Johnson, David Whiteman, and Jeffrey Zinn. 2004. *CRS Report for Congress.* Congressional Research Service, Library of Congress.

Waterman, Laura. 2003. "On Writing Wilderness Ethics: Some Further Musings of the 'Spirit of Wildness.'" *International Journal of Wilderness* 9, no. 2 (August).

Waterman, Laura, and Guy Waterman. 1993. *Wilderness Ethics: Preserving the Spirit of Wildness.* Woodstock, VT: Countryman Press.

Watson, Alan E. 2004. Human Relationships with Wilderness: The Fundamental Definition of Wilderness Character. *International Journal of Wilderness* 10, no. 3 (December).

White, Lynn, Jr. 1967. "The Historical Roots of Our Ecological Crisis." *Science* 155 (March 10).

Wilfong, Tara. 2005. "Management of National Forests." *Forest Service Centennial Magazine.*

Williams, Terry Tempest. Statement before the senate Subcommittee on Forest and Public Lands Management regarding the Utah Public Lands Management Act of 1995. Washington DC, July 13, 1995.

Winks, Robert W. 1997. "The National Park Service Act of 1916: A Contradictory Mandate?" *Denver University Law Review* 74, no. 3.

Woods, Mark. "Federal Wilderness Preservation in the United States: The Preservation of Wilderness?" in *The Great New Wilderness Debate*, ed. J. Baird Callicott and Michael P. Nelson. 1998. Athens, GA: University of Georgia Press.

Zaslowsky, Dylan, and the Wilderness Society. 1986. *These American Lands.* New York: Henry Holt and Company.

INTERNET RESOURCES

Aldo Leopold Wilderness Research Institute
http://leopold.wilderness.net/

Arthur Carhart National Wilderness Training Center
http://carhart.wilderness.net/

Bureau of Land Management www.blm.gov

Center for Environmental Philosophy
www.cep.unt.edu/

Ecology Hall of Fame www.ecotopia.org/

Forest Service Employees for Environmental Ethics
www.fseee.org/

High Country News www.hcn.org

International Association for Environmental Philosophy
www.environmentalphilosophy.org/
International Journal of Wilderness ijw.wilderness.net/
International Society for Environmental Ethics
www.cep.unt.edu/ISEE.html
Izaak Walton League of America www.iwla.org/
Leave No Trace Center for Outdoor Ethics www.lnt.org
Library of Congress: The Evolution of the Conservation
Movement
lcweb2.loc.gov/ammem/amrvhtml/conshome.html
National Outdoor Leadership School www.nols.edu
National Park Service www.nps.gov
Natural Resources Defense Council www.nrdc.org/
United Nations Educational, Scientific and Cultural
Organization (UNESCO): World Network of Bios-
phere Reserves www.unesco.org/mab/wnbr.htm
United Nations Environment Programme
www.unep.org/
University of Idaho: Wilderness Archives
www.lib.uidaho.edu/special-collections/Wilder-
ness.Archives.html
USDA Forest Service www.fs.fed.us
USDA Forest Service: Rocky Mountain Research Station
www.fs.fed.us/rm/
U.S. Department of the Interior www.doi.gov
U.S. Department of the Interior University
www.doiu.nbc.gov
U.S. Fish and Wildlife Service www.fws.gov/
Wilderness.net www.wilderness.net/
WILD Foundation www.wild.org/
World Conservation Union www.iucn.org/

Index